BETTER!

Self Help
For The
<u>Rest</u> of Us

Terry Lancaster

Para mis cuatro Marias

TABLE OF CONTENTS

JUST BE BETTER   1
Your Life Will Never Be Perfect. But You Have The Right,
The Responsibility And The Resources To Make It Better.

TAKE ACTION   21
The Only Way To Do It Is To Do It.

BE GRATEFUL   41
Expectations Are The Enemy Of Happiness, But Gratitude
Is Its BFF.

FUEL THE MACHINE   59
Real Food. Clean Water. Fresh Air And Sunshine.
Everything Else Is Optional.

TRAIN THE MACHINE   83
Quit Trying To Get Into Better Shape And Just Be The
Shape You're In Better.

GET YOUR HEAD OUT OF YOUR HEAD   103
Quit Letting An Imaginary There And Then Screw Up A
Perfectly Good Here And Now.

BE HERE NOW   117
Live Every Moment Of Your Life Like It's Your Full Time Job.

LET IT GO   137
Don't Worry About A Thing, 'Cause Every Little Thing
Gonna Be Alright.

CONNECT WIDELY & WISELY   157
Opportunities Emerge From Connections.

IT'S NOT ABOUT YOU   179
The Story You Tell The World Changes The World.

TERRY LANCASTER

ABOUT THE AUTHOR

Terry Lancaster is an author, speaker, and entrepreneur.

He writes and speaks on the power of habit and focus, helping people build better lives, one better decision at a time. He is a TEDx speaker, and his articles have appeared in multiple forums, including *The Good Men Project.*

He is co-founder and VP of Making Sh!t Happen at Instant Events Automotive Advertising. For the last 20 years he's been producing the biggest, loudest car dealer commercials in the history of big, loud car dealer commercials, most of that time working from home in his underwear.

Born and raised in Nashville, TN, he holds a degree in English/Journalism from Tennessee Technological University, where he learned how to program ginormous room-sized computers using a deck of cards and a rubber band, and how to edit newspaper and radio ads using a ruler, a razor blade, and scotch tape. And while all of that may make him sound MacGyver cool, it hasn't come in handy much since graduation.

Along with his wife of 28 years, Terry is the proud parent of three daughters and spends most of his free time, like every other middle-aged, overweight, native southerner, at the ice rink playing hockey.

Connect with Terry

on Twitter: @TerryLancaster
on Facebook: Facebook.com/Terry.Lancaster.1
on LinkedIn: LinkedIn.com/in/TerryLLancaster
via email: T@TerryLancaster.com
Read more at TerryLancaster.com

ACKNOWLEDGMENTS

For writing to be such lonely work, it sure does take a lot of people to bring a book into this world.

First off, I want to thank my wife, Mary Lancaster, and our three daughters, Jordan, Mary Margaret, and Callie Lancaster, for living through this adventure with me. They're the reason I wrote the book. Hell, they're the reason I'm on the planet.

Thanks to my dad, Glenn Lancaster, and my mom, Rosie Krapf. They are my heroes and my inspiration. There was never a time in my childhood that they didn't have three jobs between them. Their hard work and sacrifices gave me the opportunity to grow into the man I eventually became.

My name is the only one on the cover, but I did not do this by myself. Thanks to my editors, Chris Murray and Thomas Fiffer. Thanks to my business partner and brother-in-arms, Jeff Lee. He's the one who made the cover art pop. He's been making my words look pretty for two decades now. Thanks to my friends, Bob Brown, Cliff Curtis, Jeff Cotten, Richy Long, and Paul Wise for their work on the book trailer. My marketing coach, Dave Delaney, kept me on point and on track through the whole process.

Thanks to all my hockey-slash-used-to-be-drinking buddies on the BEER and Iceholes teams for joining in my shenanigans and for putting up with me in these last few, mostly shenanigan-free, years. A special thanks to Craig Daliessio for setting the example, showing me that this was even a possibility, and for pushing me to become what I wasn't entirely sure I wanted to be.

And thanks to you, whoever you are, for reading these words. Much of the time I spent writing this book, I felt like a crazy person alone in a room muttering to myself. Your eyeballs looking at these words makes me feel slightly more sane.

Giddyup.

Perfection Is An Illusion Created By Marketers
To Sell More Hair Care Products.

1. Just Be Better

Your Life Will Never Be Perfect. But You Have The Right,
The Resources, And The Responsibility To Make It Better.

I got up at 5 o'clock in the morning and ran across the Golden Gate Bridge.

Anyone who has known me for any length of time knows what a ridiculous sentence that is. Every word of it is true. It's still ridiculous.

I had spent the day before at the largest convention in the automotive business. Wandering around by myself, in corners, in hallways, and in single tiny slivers of sunlight I could find. Rehearsing the speech I was slated to deliver that afternoon in front of a couple hundred car dealers and automotive reporters.

This was the culmination of two years preparation and training. And the first time in my life I had taken the stage to speak in front of a group of people there specifically to hear me. To hear what I had to say and how I could help them.

I stepped to the lectern, waited for the canned audio intro to finish, and tossed fistfuls of dollars in the air as I proceeded to tell the dealers in attendance how to better spend the hundreds of thousands of dollars they each spent on advertising last year.

Once the speech was given, I could relax and enjoy my trip to San Francisco. My wife, Mary, and I got up dark and early the next morning and took an Uber out to the Golden Gate Bridge, where we were planning to meet a group of folks from the convention and from the #LiveALittle Project. We ended up under the bridge by a closed cafe and had to scramble up the hill, hand over fist half a mile or so before we could even start across the bridge.

We walked across the bridge completely in the dark. I'm not totally comfortable with heights, so walking 250 feet above the water in the dark was freaking me out a little, and I was staying far enough to the left to irritate the bicyclists passing by.

Mary turned around and walked back across at a leisurely pace and ended up catching some great pictures of the sunrise on the bay.

And I ran.

Slowly. Slower than a thundering herd of turtles in a peanut butter swamp. But I was running. At many points both my feet were off the ground. That makes it running--officially.

I ran the entire span of the bridge. 1.7 miles. No stopping. No walking. No Puking.

Me.

It still doesn't make any sense to me how that happened. If anyone had ever suggested that I'd be up at the ass crack of dawn, running across a bridge in California, I would have flat out told you, "Your cornbread ain't done. Your elevator does not go all the way to the top. You ain't right."

The only way you'd catch me running across a bridge in the dark was if someone were chasing me.

For one thing, 5 o'clock has always been a lot closer to bedtime for me than morning time.

I've always been a night owl. When I was a kid, I would hear my dad's alarm clock go off (around 5:00 am) and I'd quickly turn off the TV, jump into bed, and hide under the covers so he wouldn't know I'd been up all night. I don't think he fell for it.

For most of my adult life, crawling into bed around 5:00 am was not an entirely rare occurrence: the bars close at 3:00, and Steak 'n Shake is open 24 hours a day.

I thought my night-owlish ways were genetic. Built into my DNA. Hardwired. Something that was out of my control.

Then there's the running. It wasn't that long ago that I couldn't run to the mailbox without stopping to catch my breath. I'd never, ever run farther than a mile. And I hadn't done that since high school.

In junior high school, I was the fat kid struggling to run the field after football practice, stopping to walk whenever I was reasonably sure Coach wasn't watching.

I thought being fat and out of shape was who I was. Genetic. Hardwired in. Core.

And of course the drinking.

I was a drinking man long before I was actually a man. I started on the booze when I was 14 years old and drank with enthusiasm for decades. If there was anything about me that I thought was truly immutable it was this--I liked to party. I wore it like a badge of honor.

My grandfather was a drinking man before me. I used to tell all my drinking buddies about how every once in awhile Granddaddy would swear off the hard stuff and only drink beer for a while (drinkers are always making such little bargains). Granddaddy would be ok for while and then he'd go from beer to malt liquor. And then eventually, he'd slip the sixer of Schlitz into the freezer and just drink the pure liquor out of the can when everything else froze. He kept his promise, but he drank himself into an early grave.

I thought drinking was genetic. Fundamental. Hardwired in.

I'm pretty much a homebody. Not much of a world traveler. Before running the bridge, I'd never been to California. I've spent 99.9% of my breathing hours within a couple of hundred miles of the dingy hospital where I was born on the banks of the Cumberland River in downtown Nashville.

Most days now, I don't even bother to put on pants, much less leave the house.

But a couple of days after I ran the Golden Gate Bridge, there I was flying back from California on a 787 Dreamliner.

"This Is Where I Leave You" was playing on the inflight entertainment system, and one of the characters spoke this line:

"Anything can happen. Anything happens all the time."

And it does. And it can.

The transformation in my life over the last few years is actually a little surreal. I'm not entirely sure how it all happened. Yes, I've made better decisions. I'm still not a morning person. But most days now, I'm up and at 'em a couple hours earlier than I used to be, getting shit done.

I run every day. Rain or shine. Hell or high water.

I'm up earlier, exercising every morning, in part because I'm not hungover. I haven't had a drink in years.

Still, when I started dragging my fat ass around the block in Tennessee, I could have never imagined running across the Golden Gate Bridge in California. It wasn't something in the realm of possibility.

But it happened. The impossible happens all the time.

And forgive me if I get a little hippy dippy on you for just a minute, but here's what I think I've learned.

Anything really can happen. The universe is made out of infinite possibilities. Everything you can imagine and amazing things that you could never imagine in a hundred years of imagining are all swirling around in a giant cloud of uncertainty just waiting for you to will them into existence.

Life is an amazing, never ending series of Miracles just waiting for you to set them in motion.

Transformation really is possible.

Even for people like you. Even for people like me.

Ordinary people like us can create extraordinary lives for ourselves. *Starting where we are. Using what we have.*

The life you were born to lead doesn't look like it does in the commercials. And it doesn't come in box, in pill form or with an easy button. But if you're willing to work for it, it can be yours one minor adjustment at a time.

Every self-proclaimed self help guru has a story about when they hit rock bottom. Where they were at before they turned their life around. Infomercial superstar Don Lapre was living in a tiny one-bedroom apartment when he learned how to make a fortune with classified ads.

And then there's Chris Farley's motivational mastermind Matt Foley striving to make something of himself while living in a van down by the river.

Everyone's got a van down by the river story. Here's mine:

I was working part time as a bartender. Now I wasn't a bartender by trade. I owned what had been a successful ad agency, but the ad business had fallen on hard times and I was tending bar at concerts and sporting events to help keep the wheels on the bus.

Garth Brooks was doing a series of comeback concerts, something like 12 sold-out shows in seven days in Nashville, taping them for a network special. He hadn't toured in about a decade, so it was kind of a big deal.

I was working behind the counter with a friend of mine from England who had only lived in the states for a few years and honestly had no idea who Garth Brooks was or why he had 12 sold-out shows. I was explaining that during the 80's and 90's Garth Brooks had sold more records than any human--alive or dead--more records than Elvis and the Beatles.

Then she asked me, "How old is he?"

And I answered, without pause, "He's our age. Like 50 or so."

"Like 50."

As soon as I said it, it was like someone had kicked me in the groin. I was about to be 50 freaking years old!

My friend even noticed my sudden change in demeanor, or maybe it was just the color rushing from my face.

I was a less than a handful of years away from turning the big 5-0.

My business, which had been my entire self identity for a long time, was on the verge of failing.

I was a happy meal shy of 300 pounds. And I drank too much.

My shit was fucked up.

It occurred to me in that flash of a moment (epiphany is the big boy word) that if I didn't get my shit together, and soon, it was probably gonna be fucked up for a long time to come.

About the only hobby I've ever had, other than working and drinking, was playing ice hockey. I was already one of the oldest players playing rec league hockey. But I knew a few guys who had played into their 50s, 60s, even 70s.

My personal hero, Jerry Franz, played hockey in Nashville well into his 70s. But here's the thing: Jerry was a lean, mean hockey machine. He worked out, ran triathlons, and took a lot better care of himself than I did.

Nobody was skating around the ice at 300 pounds into their 50s and 60s much less their 70s.

If I didn't start taking better care of myself, I wasn't going to be playing hockey much longer.

If I didn't get myself turned around I was gonna be Matt Foley--fat, broke, and living in a van down by the river.

There's a scene in *Animal House* where Dean Wormer gathers the men of Delta Tau Chi in his office and tells them that "Fat, drunk, and stupid is no way to go through life."

I had spent most of my life trying to prove him wrong. Or at least that two out of three wasn't bad.

Now, if this were one of Don Lapre's infomercials, I'd tell you how I went out and placed one little tiny classified ad that solved all my financial problems. How I discovered a secret fruit milkshake that tasted like Godiva Chocolate and helped me lose 100 pounds in 3 months. How I invented a workout program that only took 10 minutes a day and gave me rock hard abs without ever doing a single sit up.

That's not the way it worked out.

In real life, people don't go from a van down by the river to a mansion on the hill. At least not overnight.

But something had to change. Hell, a lot of things had to change. And the thing that needed changing most was me.

I started exercising a little. Walking around the block at first. Then running. And by running I mean jogging, more like a cross between a trot and a shuffle. The first day I tried to run, I was tired by the time I got to the mailbox, but I was determined to make it 100 yards to the stop sign at the corner of my street.

Close, but no cigar.

Then, one day, at the age of 48, I ran a mile non-stop for the first time since I was teenager. Then I ran two. Then 3! You should have seen me that day shuffling down the street with my fists in air belting out the theme from Rocky at the top of my lungs.

I still run so slow that buzzards follow me home, but every day, I'm out running around my neighborhood.

I started changing my eating habits a little at a time. Going from four spoons of sugar in my coffee to three then two then one then none--straight black, no cream, no chaser.

I started treating sugar as a drug, and I learned to use food as fuel, not as entertainment.

Then I accidentally quit drinking. I liked to drink, but I took a 30-day vacation from booze and it just kinda stuck.

The first time anyone ever mentioned the idea of me writing a book about self improvement, I laughed and told them that I was going to write a book and call it "How to Lose a Hundred Pounds and Make a Million Dollars."

Only I had to lose a hundred pounds and make a million dollars first.

I haven't done either of those things, but here I sit, writing the book anyway because along the way I figured something out that's more important than losing a hundred pounds.

More important than making a million dollars.

Something more powerful than money and beauty.

They don't teach this in school, and the talking heads on TV never get around to mentioning it.

I don't need to lose a hundred pounds to be healthy. I don't need a million dollars to be happy. I don't need perfectly whitened teeth or granite countertops. I don't need any of that shit. And neither do you.

I'm sorry if you bought this book thinking I was going to teach you some ancient Egyptian secret for attracting money, beauty, and perfection into your life. But the truth is, you're probably never going to be a millionaire. You're probably never going to be a movie star, run a marathon, or have a perfect set of six-pack abs.

But here's the good news: It doesn't matter.

You don't need those things. You don't need perfection to live a better life. You can be healthier. You can be happier. And you can be more prosperous.

You can be better. And you can start right now.

But first you have to let go of the relentless pursuit of perfection. You're never going to be perfect. There's no such thing. Perfect doesn't exist in nature.

Perfection is an illusion created by marketers to sell us hair care products.

And perfect is an obstacle. Every day we let the siren song of perfection get in the way of us living perfectly great lives. We keep waiting around, hoping for perfect, settling for average, and worshipping the glimpses of excellence we see in others.

As a culture, we love heroes. Champions. Gold Medal Winners. We're obsessed with winning. With being best. Or, more often than not, watching and cheering as someone else crosses the finish line. We've let cheers for our heroes and champions turn us into spectators.

We've let our cultural obsession with the best in others blind us to the awesome power of just being a little better ourselves.

Human beings are built for continuous, incremental improvement.

If you've ever sat through a sales presentation from a financial planner, you've no doubt heard the tale of the Sultan and The Chessboard.

An ancient Sultan, King, Ruler, or Grand Poobah of some faraway land decided to honor one of his priests and grant him one wish.

"Your Grand Poobahness," said the priest. "I am but your humble servant. I ask simply for single grain of rice on the first square of a chessboard today. For that to be doubled on the second square on the second day, doubled again on the third day and so on till all of the squares are filled."

The Grand Poobah was amused by the simplicity of the request and scoffed at the priest.

"I am the Great and Mighty Poobah. I could grant you gold and jewels and riches beyond measure and you ask for rice from the granary. I scoff at you and grant your silly wish."

The first month went by fine, but soon it became apparent that the Priest had outwitted the Poobah, and there was not enough rice in all the land to grant his wish. Then, depending on which version of the story you hear, the Priest becomes the new Poobah, or the Poobah chops the Priest's head off and goes back to eating grapes and fornicating.

We don't count our riches in rice, so let's put that in dollars and cents. If each grain of rice were replaced with a single penny, by the time the chessboard was filled the Poobah would have been out $185 QUADRILLION. That's 185 followed by 15 zeros!

Financial planners use this story to illustrate the truly mind- blowing power of compound interest. How saving and investing small amounts today can yield gigantic results later. And countless books, from *Get Rich Slow* to *The Millionaire Next Door*, point out that riches don't often come in tidal waves, but in trickles ... one drop at time.

But that's not the story that makes the evening news. We like to hear tales of 20-year-olds who drop out of college to start the latest and greatest technology companies and sell out for billions in an IPO a couple of years later. We like lottery winners and first-round draft picks who buy their Momma a new Ferrari. We like our rags to riches stories fast and furious.

And not just with money. The guy who drops 20 pounds and lowers his blood pressure and blood sugar doesn't make the news.

The woman who goes from watching TV all night, every night to walking around the block after dinner doesn't get her own reality show, but we pile around the screens watching THE BIGGEST LOSER contestants fight to sweat and puke their way to a 100-pound weight loss in a month or two.

Never mind that that rapid weight loss is both unhealthy and unsustainable.

Never mind that lottery winners are surprisingly destitute and depressed within a few years of winning the lottery, and first round draft picks are usually broke and out of the league before Momma gets the hang of throttle steering her Italian pony.

Whether we're seeking to improve our finances, our health, our business, or anything else, our lottery winner, gold medal, blue ribbon mentality keeps us swinging for the fences and sets us up for endless cycles of failure and despondence. Diet and gain. Profit and Loss.

Sustainable change is almost always incremental change.

Gretchen Rubin from *The Happiness Project* says the things we do every day affect our lives more than the things we do every once in awhile.

A little bit of effort every day matters many times more than the grandest of plans and good intentions.

Aristotle said "We are what we repeatedly do. Excellence, then, is not an act, but a habit."

If we're seeking to make lasting changes in our lives, we have to quit swinging for the fences, hoping to win the lottery, and concentrate on the small tasks that we can accomplish today, tomorrow and every day thereafter, tasks that we can turn into habits and habits that can turn into a lifestyle to help create the lives we were born to lead ... one chessboard square at a time.

You can have a better life. You can be better.

But hoping for it and wishing for it, talking about it, and dreaming about it, visualizing it and lighting candles, none of that stuff is going get the job done.

Reading this book doesn't count.

You have to do something about it.

You have to get up off your ass and make it happen ... a little bit at a time.

In 1940, America was braced for war. Europe was engulfed and we were sure to follow. We just weren't ready.

We didn't have the manufacturing capabilities needed to build the machinery of war. The men with the know-how to get the job done done were soon to be heading for the front lines. And the economy was still reeling from a decade long slump. Without money or manpower, we couldn't count on new factories or great leaps forward in innovation.

We had to get better and we had to get better fast.

The department of war created programs to consult with important industries who were being challenged by the loss of manpower and the flurry of demand. One of the training programs encouraged manufacturers to *NOT* place their efforts into radical, innovative techniques to meet these new challenges.

Instead they should should concentrate on continuous improvement.

"Look for hundreds of small things you can do to improve. Don't try to plan a whole new department or go after the big installation of

new equipment. There isn't time for these major items. Look for improvements on existing jobs with your present equipment."

Do what you can with what you have. Right now. Right where you are.

This strategy must have seemed like so much tilting at windmills in the face of Germany's warring and manufacturing prowess. We were pitting the lowly suggestion box against German Panzer tanks.

Little by little, though, we got better. Our speed of production increased. Our quality control improved. We shipped men and machines halfway around the world and secured the economic dominance the US has enjoyed for the last 70 years.

Meanwhile in Japan, after the war, their manufacturing capability had been destroyed. Completely.

General Douglas MacArthur was commander of the occupation forces in postwar Japan, and he needed a strong economy, especially transportation and manufacturing sectors, to bolster his forces against the looming Communist threat in China and North Korea. Japan was too vital to leave in a weakened state.

MacArthur saw the same dire need for manufacturing improvement that the Department of War had seen in the U.S. economy in 1940. So he brought in the same programs to solve Japan's biggest problems one little problem at a time.

As the Japanese economy bounced from the post war years when "Made In Japan" was an insult and a trade barrier to the 1980's when Japanese manufacturing and management techniques were the toast of the corporate and financial worlds, the decidedly American management philosophy of continuous improvement became ingrained into the Japanese business culture as the concept of KAIZEN.

Kaizen is widely credited with the Japanese economic miracle of the late 20th Century.

And American re-adaptation of these "Japanese" techniques in the 80s and 90s helped the quality turnaround in US manufacturing. When Ford marketing people noticed that consumers were requesting Japanese- made engines, even though they were built on the exact same specs as the American-made engine, their engineers found that, while all of the engines were built to spec and within the allowed tolerances, the Japanese engines were built to within tolerances twice as exacting, 1/16 of an inch as opposed to the required 1/8.

American companies had faced little competition in the postwar years and had seen little need for continuous improvement. Those days were over.

These days, management consultants say there are two strategies for creating change:

Innovation--radical reform and drastic measures attempting to achieve one-time, orders of magnitude size improvement.

Kaizen--continuous improvement in all areas, using minor adjustments to achieve slight, ever-increasing positive results.

We face the same choice creating change in our personal lives.

It's easy to swing for the fences and look for the one magic bullet: the mystical weight loss program, the miracle diet, the thermogenic califragilistic workout system that can triple our metabolism and cut our body fat in half.

We're looking for radical change, the one saving grace that will at long last turn our lives around.

But there is no magic bullet.

There is no miracle diet.

There is no great innovation that's going to change the life you're living now into the life that you were born to lead.

There's only you. And the hundreds, thousands of decisions you make every day. And the simple truth that if you can start making just a few of those decisions, better decisions, then you can change your life in ways you've never dreamed.

Start here. Start Now. Start Small.

Just Start.

Since that night in Nashville, with the smell of stale beer all around me and Garth Brooks wailing about friends in low places in the background, I've dropped about 60 pounds. And I don't want to oversell anything. I'm still a fat ass. But I'm in the best shape of my life. And yes, round is a shape.

But losing 60 pounds is, honestly, the least important benefit of the changes I've made in my life.

Business is good. A lot of that is thanks to the economy. But if I hadn't righted the ship, got the oars back in the water, and repaired the sail no amount of rising tide was going to get my struggling business back afloat. I'd be just as broke today, probably broker. The changes I made saved my business.

And for that I'm incredibly grateful. But that's still not the best part.

The huge benefit of the changes I've made is that I've changed the way I think--about almost everything.

And changing the way I think has changed the way I feel.

My friends ask me how I feel since I've lost the weight. And I tell 'em, "I feel freaking fantastic."

I feel like a superhero. I feel like I could shoot fire out of my fingertips if I really wanted to.

People who know about horses and dogs are always looking at their teeth and nails to judge how healthy they are. I look at my fingernails now and they're almost embarrassingly pink. I'm afraid people are going to start asking me if I'm painting them.

I've got more energy. More stamina. More money.

I'm a better hockey player than I've ever been. And I'm just plain happier.

I'm a better me and that's the story I want to tell.

The story about the minor adjustments I made to my life, which snowballed into lifestyle changes which helped me drop the weight, get off the booze, make more money, and learn to be happy.

I want to tell people, regular people, every day on the block people, people struggling just to make it to the end of another day: You can turn your life around.

No matter how old you are. No matter how fat you are. No matter how broke you are.

If you're ready to make a change in your life, you don't need to run a marathon tomorrow. All you have to do is get your dead ass up off the couch and take the first step today.

You CAN create the life you were born to lead, one minor adjustment at a time.

ACTION STEPS

Throughout the book, I'll be giving you specific action steps that you can take on the road to BETTER! because knowledge without action is just entertainment. We'll get into the hows and whys later, but for now, if you'll get up and do these 10 things RIGHT NOW, build them into daily habits, even if you never get around to reading the rest of the book, your life will be better and my work will be complete.

Giddyup!

1) STAND UP. Straight as you can and raise your arms to the ceiling as high as you can. Stay there for about a minute. Don't forget to breathe. Jazz Fingers!

2) STRETCH. This way and that way. Back and forth. Bend over and stretch. Touch your toes if you can, and wave at them if you can't. And if you can't even see them, just imagine what they're gonna look like when you get there because you will get there.

3) GO FOR A WALK. Preferably outside. To the mailbox, around the block, around the parking lot. It doesn't matter how far. It doesn't matter how fast. Just get up and get moving.

4) CLOSE YOUR EYES AND BREATHE. Breathe in, breathe out. For just one minute, try not to think about anything but the breath you are taking. In through your nose, out through your mouth. And when something else pops in your head, because it will, accept it and go back to thinking about your breath.

5) DRINK A GLASS OF WATER. A nice big glass of pure, crystal clear water. Clean water to drink and clean air to breathe are the only two things you need from this world to make it through today. Everything else is optional.

6) SEND SOMEONE A THANK YOU NOTE. Somewhere, someone has done something nice for you today. Something that made your world a little better. Start exercising your appreciation bone and say thanks!

7) CALL YOUR MOM. and tell her you love her. Or your dad or your grandparents. Or your great aunt. Or your spouse. Or your kids. Anyone that you know will be happy to hear those words. You have the power to make other people happy. You should totally do that more.

8) EAT A VEGETABLE. You remember what they look like, right? They're usually by the front door of the supermarket. Maybe you didn't notice them because they don't come in a colorful box. They also don't have an ingredient list. Eat more stuff like that.

9) TIDY UP. If you're at home, make your bed. If you're at work, clean your desk. Look around you right now, wherever you are, and clean it up. If it belongs somewhere else, put it somewhere else. If you don't need it, trash it, recycle it or give it away. And here's the big secret--You probably don't need it.

10) BREAK A SWEAT. Do some jumping jacks, high knees, or running in place as hard as you can for a minute or so. Being BETTER! is hard work, and if you thought it was going to happen without you ever breaking a sweat, well, you were wrong.

For more info on kaizen and continuous improvement visit TerryLancaster.com/JustBeBetter.

A Journey Of A Thousand Miles Begins With A Single Step.

2. Take Action

—

The Only Way To Do It Is To Do It.

—

You cheated didn't you?

You jumped right from Chapter 1 to Chapter 2 without taking a break to do any of the activities.

Oh, I understand. I'm a gifted, talented writer (and a damn handsome man, to boot). My words have reeled you in and you just can't wait for my next pearl of wisdom. I'm flattered.

But there isn't a single word in this book that's going to make your life the tiniest bit better.

That's all on you.

You can read every self help book ever written. You can watch all the videos. You can put Tony Robbins and Deepak Chopra on speed dial. You can talk about getting better. You can dream about getting better. You can visualize being better and build a 17-point plan for turning your life around. But at the end of the day, nothing is ever going to change until you get up and do something.

You can't change your life without changing your lifestyle.

Nothing will ever change until you do.

You wanna lose weight. Get a better job. Be nicer to your kids. Drink less. Exercise more.

That's a wish list. A shopping list.

It's like we opened up the Toys "R" Us Sale Flyer and picked out all the perfect accessories for The New and Improved ME DOLL, now with Kung Fu Grip.

We want to be be better than we are. Thinner. Richer. Happier. More This. Less That. Better.

That's the easy part. Wanting it.

We know what we want or think we do anyway. We can make a list.

What we don't do for the most part is DO anything about it

We keep waiting for the New Job Fairy to come bring us an exciting new adventure and a couple of bucks under the pillow. We're waiting for the Cellulite Bunny to come wiggle his nose and take that extra 15 to 20 pounds of lard off our round mound of rebound.

But, deep down inside, we all know there is no New Job Fairy and the Cellulite Bunnies are long since extinct.

The only way any of those things are going to happen is if we make them happen.

So here's the new plan and it only has one point:

Get your dead ass up and make it happen.

Wanna lose weight? Exercise More and Eat Less.

Wanna Make More Money? Work Harder. Send Out More Resumes. Call More Customers. Knock on More Doors.

We've been so conditioned to think about the bottom line, the end result, winning the prize, that we only think about the outcomes: how much weight have I lost, how many inches did I add to my bicep, how much money did I make.

But thinking about outcomes does almost nothing to affect real change.

We have to think more about the inputs: what am I DOING that will help me lose weight; what am I DOING to build my biceps; what am I DOING to make more money.

It's all about the action, baby!

Before Sugar Ray Leonard became a six-time world champion professional boxer, before he won the Gold Medal, before he was elected to the Boxing Hall of Fame, before he pocketed over $100 million in purses, and yes, even before "Dancing With The Stars," before all of that Sugar Ray Leonard was just Ray, a scrawny teenager outside Washington, DC, with a big dream and the determination and work ethic that make dreams come true.

Everyday Ray would wake up, get dressed, and walk his younger siblings to the bus stop for school, but when his brothers and sisters got on the bus along with all his friends, he waited and watched as the bus doors closed and the bus pulled off. Then with everyone staring out the back of the bus at him, he'd reach down, tighten his sneakers and start to run, chasing the bus to school everyday.

"The other kids thought I was crazy," Leonard said, "because I would run in the rain, snow--it didn't matter. I did it because I didn't just want to be better than the next guy, I wanted to be better than all the guys."

At the age of 16, he lied about his age to be allowed to participate in the Olympic tryouts.

Sugar Ray didn't WANT to be a great boxer. Sugar Ray didn't HOPE for success. DREAM about it. WISH for it. Or WAIT for some rich and famous boxing authority to come along and tap him on the shoulder to be the next big thing.

And he didn't build a dream board full of pictures of famous boxers and all the bright and shiny things he was going to buy with his $100 Million in prize money.

Sugar Ray got up everyday, put his running shoes on, and made that shit happen.

Sugar Ray worked his ass off because ...

Working your ass off is what makes dreams come true.

No one has ever had to tell my buddy Scott Scovill to shit or get off the pot. When it's time to go, Scott goes.

Scott is one of the most successful entrepreneurs in the entertainment business, logging hundreds of thousands of frequent flyer miles a year touring and shuttling between his companies in Nashville and Los Angeles.

In Nashville his Moo TV handles video content creation for country music superstars like Alan Jackson and Brad Paisley. In Los

Angeles, his company CenterStaging is consistently ranked as the top rehearsal facility for touring artists.

And as if all that weren't enough, on his days off he's a world class photographer, directs videos, and plays a little beer league hockey with me on the side--oh, and he travels to places like Antarctica and Russia just for shits and giggles.

Twenty years ago, Scott was none of that. He was a struggling college student, failing out of school with a zero point zero GPA, waiting tables at Howard Johnson's and working odd jobs to stay afloat.

But a chance encounter and Scott's massive, determined action turned it all around.

The road crew from U2's Joshua Tree tour happened into the Howard Johnson's in Albany, New York and sat down at one of Scott's tables. They hit it off and invited him to the show, one of the very first to feature extensive use of video.

Scott describes that show as a paradigm shift. He saw clearly that the combination of entertainment and technology was a much better future than a series of dead end jobs and failing out of school. So he quit.

Quit school. Quit his jobs. Quit everything and followed the tour to the next town to see how he could help. And then he followed them to the next town. And then he sold his car and all his worldly possessions and went on the road for good.

He didn't sit around talking about it.

He didn't spend months on end agonizing over the decision.

He didn't brag at parties about how one day he was going to go on the road with rock stars.

He got his ass up and took massive, determined action. Right Then. Right There.

Because the only way to do it is to do it.

Time and success haven't changed his style.

When downtown Nashville flooded in 2010, the newscasts were filled with stories about musicians who had lost all of their concert riggings and equipment in the flood. It made for good TV, but it wasn't entirely accurate because all of that equipment didn't belong to the country music superstars. They rented it ... from Scott.

Millions and millions of dollars worth of electronics and video equipment were destroyed. And he never batted an eye. In fact it was probably close to a year later before he had an accurate estimate of the losses.

He was too busy working and rebuilding to stop and count.

He doubled down with even more massive, determined action.

It's how he plays beer league hockey too. As with me, no one has ever accused Scott Scovill of being a naturally gifted athlete, but what he is is an eighth of a ton of sheer determination. A bull in a china shop is not nearly a strong enough metaphor.

But that's OK.

Determination, action, and good old-fashioned hard work trump talent and planning any day of the week.

In 1971 Julius Erving wasn't just a giant in college basketball, he was literally playing a different game, singlehandedly inventing the modern, above-the-rim style while earthbound mortals could only stand by and watch.

During his two seasons at the University of Massachusetts, Erving, better known as Dr. J, **AVERAGED** over 30 points and 20 rebounds per game.

In January of 1971, The UMass Redmen were 11-1 and hadn't lost a game on their home floor in over a year when Digger Phelps brought his Fordham Rams into The Cage, UMass's legendary arena in Amherst.

Phelps's squad was a ragtag collection of Irish and Italian kids from Brooklyn and the Bronx. They had little height to begin with, and their tallest player had gone down weeks before with a season-ending injury. Most of the other players stood little above 6 feet tall, and none had the gravity defying skills of Erving. They never stood a chance.

Or did they?

Fordham came out in a full court press from the opening buzzer, swarming Erving and the other Redmen like hornets, never conceding an inch of ground, battling for every ball.

"It was unbelievable how they covered ground," says basketball coaching legend Rick Pitino, who was a freshman riding the bench for UMass during that game.

Phelps sent one scrappy New York kid after another to guard Erving. And one after another they fouled out, but Dr. J was contained and Fordham won the game 87-79.

"There's no way they should have beaten us," says Pitino. "Nobody beat us at The Cage."

Hard work works. And we know that.

Taking action gets things done.

The problem is us.

We've spent our entire lifetime receiving the gospel of NO PAIN, NO GAIN, and we don't like pain so we avoid it as long as possible.

We recognize the value of action, but we want to make sure that we're totally ready and that if we're actually gonna take all this action, we're taking the right action so we plan and schedule and mentally prepare ourselves for the big new workout plan we're going to start next week.

For the trendy new diet we're going to start on the first of the month.

To stop smoking tomorrow.

To double down on our work efforts and get more shit done next quarter.

And we plan so hard we rarely get around to the actual doing.

We put it off and put it off and put it off. And build up all these expectations in our head that this time, this time it's actually going to work. THIS is the magic bullet that's going to fix us.

We've ordered the perfect workout clothes. Bought the magic juicing blender that captures every ounce of nutrients and only half the carbs. Installed the home gym/Rube Goldberg contraption that burns twice the calories in half time.

And then we actually DO THE THING.

That one time.

Maybe two.

But it doesn't live up to our expectations. It doesn't change our lives overnight. WTF?

Our lives are a wreck and we want to fix it NOW. We want to be rich and famous, with six-pack abs, 2.3 children, and a loving spouse. And we want it all now. We deserve it all NOW!

We've spent all this money, watched all these DVDs, worked so hard (that one time, maybe twice) for what? To lose one pound? Why bother?

So we go back to the couch. The couch understands. The couch is our friend.

And we decide we just don't have enough motivation, enough willpower to see it through, so we log on to Pinterest to read Zig Ziglar quotes or maybe we go out and buy another book, like this one, to give us that little extra motivational push that we need.

But motivation isn't the problem. I've been motivated to lose weight my whole life.

The problem is that concentrating on the end results raises our expectations.

And expectations are the enemy of happiness.

Stanford Professor B.J. Fogg has developed a formula to express exactly what affects our behaviors. Motivation (how much we want it) turns out to be only one leg of the stool.

Behavior = (Motivation x Ability) + Trigger

When it comes to behavior, motivation is intricately related to ability (how difficult something is for us). Motivation decreases according to how difficult the behavior is.

We may want to run a marathon, save for retirement, and rebuild the '71 Cutlass sitting in our garage, but if those things don't come easy for us, our brains will make the decision to pick up the remote instead of picking up the wrench, and we'll be back in front of the tube for the long haul.

Relying primarily on motivation to change your behavior long term is a losing strategy.

So Fogg developed a three-step system he calls "Tiny Habits" for changing behavior that minimizes the impact of motivation and relies on the other two legs of the stool.

1) Start small.

Really small. So small it seems downright silly.

Like writing one sentence.

Like doing one push up

Like marching in place during one 30-second commercial.

He wants you to start so small the activity can be done in 30 seconds or less. And the activity must cause no pain. If it's painful, your mind is going to figure out the perfect excuse to help you avoid the pain. We don't like pain.

But you'll notice that none of the activities are from the typical self-improvements wish list we all make every New Year's

Lose Weight.

Make More Money.

Get In Shape.

You know why THOSE aren't on the professor's list? Because they aren't *activities*, they're *objectives*.

You have to DO something to get something and Tiny Habits is about the doing.

Do the right thing and the right results will follow.

"Yeah, but how am I going to get in shape or lose weight doing one pushup?"

That's a valid question. And the answer is this. Success breeds success. Accomplishment creates confidence. And repetition creates aptitude.

So going back to his magic formula, every minor victory increases ability and lowers our need for higher doses of motivation.

Fogg has gone from struggling through a couple of pushups in a row to knocking out 60 or 70 in a day.

We've all started out on big life changing projects, failed, and let our goals slip to the side.

Tiny Habits advocates the polar opposite approach. Choose an activity so simple, so easy that it's virtually impossible to fail.

I read of one participant in the program who just committed to the simple act of putting on her running shoes every morning often going back to sleep after she did. But eventually, once the lacing up of the shoes became an ingrained habit, she decided that since the shoes were on anyway, she might as well go for a run.

Little changes can lead to big results.

2) Finding a trigger.

Doing one pushup isn't a magic bullet.

We all know that we should exercise more. Read more. Write more. Study harder. Make more sales calls. Eat our veggies.

We know what we're supposed to do.

My buddy, sales trainer Jim Ziegler (no relation to Zig), often says that salespeople don't have a knowing problem. They have a doing problem.

We know what to do. But most of us don't do it because we don't have motivation sufficient enough to overcome the excuses our brain throws out there.

We can listen to motivational speakers to get us through one more day and we can aim for behaviors so small that we almost have to do them. But the real mojo happens when our sporadic burst of good behaviors become deeply ingrained instincts.

We need good habits that propel us through the day and on toward our ultimate goals.

What we need is automaticity.

I've got a degree in English Journalism, and I've made a living putting words together in pleasing order for the last 30 years, but I have to admit the first time I watched Fogg's TED talk, I had to stop the video and go look up automaticity, not to understand what it meant, but just to make sure it was really a word. It is.

Automaticity (Noun) // *The ability to do things without occupying the mind with the low-level details required, allowing it to become an automatic response pattern or habit. It is usually the result of learning, repetition, and practice.*

Fogg's research had shown that we need a trigger, a call to action, to inspire us to enact behaviors, but his biggest breakthrough came while getting dressed one morning. He opened his sock drawer, removed a pair of socks, and closed the drawer without thinking, and he was struck by the power of the word AFTER.

By linking the habitual behavior we want (closing the drawer) AFTER a habitual behavior we already have (opening the drawer) we build in automaticity and complete the three legged stool-- motivation, ability, trigger.

We all have hundreds, probably thousands of tiny actions that we complete every day without thought, and we can use them as the triggers for the habits we're attempting to create.

We can program our brains just like we program a computer:

If This, Then That

Each line of Tiny Habits code, then looks something like this:

AFTER I (current habit), I will (desired tiny habit).

AFTER I open the drawer, I will close the drawer.

AFTER start the coffee machine, I will put on my running shoes.

And my personal favorite from Fogg's life which I incorporated into mine:

AFTER I pee, I will do a pushup.

Pushups have always been a problem for me. I'm built like a little teapot (short and stout), so I don't have a lot of leverage to lift my eighth of a ton up into the air. But after less than a week of doing one pushup every time I urinated, they became noticeably easier. Little wonder, I did more pushups in five days than I'd done in the previous five years, because it's simple and because, now that I had a trigger (SFX: toilet flushing), it's automatic.

3) Celebrate.

But even the magic sound of the toilet flushing wasn't enough to get my new pushup habit to stick around for good, according to Fogg. For that, we have to become addicted to the new habit. We have to crave doing a pushup or marching in place or making that one extra sales call.

And that's the easy part. Our brain has an addictive personality.

It's hardwired to release the most addictive substances on the planet--serotonin and dopamine. And all we have to do is trick our minds into thinking we're happy.

So every time we complete our tiny habit, we have to do a tiny celebration.

We can give ourselves a thumbs up.

We can say "I'm Awesome."

"Winner Winner Chicken Dinner."

Whatever it takes for our brain to recognize that we've done something worthy of celebrating and release all that happy juice.

And soon enough our brain will link the new behavior to the ensuing flood of happiness and Voila! a new habit is born.

So now it's not enough that every time I pee I drop to the floor for a pushup (No, not the bathroom floor! I go to another room).

I have to pee, drop to the floor for a pushup, then stand up and do a little happy dance, arms in the air, raising the roof "Woot! Woot!"

It's OK To start small. but you have to start now!

Life doesn't start after you turn 18, after college, after you get a job, after you get married and have kids, after the kids leave home, or after you retire. Life doesn't start a week from next Tuesday.

Life is today.

Life is what happens while you're busy making 17-point plans about how to live your life.

Life is now. And that's all there really is.

The past and the future are both figments of your imagination. If there's anything you want to do, you best be getting off your ass and start doing it. Now.

If there's something you want to be. Be it. Now.

If there's something you want to happen. It's not going to happen, unless you make it happen.

It's all, totally and completely, up to you.

If you want to write. Write. If you want to sing. Sing. If you want to travel. Hit the road.

If you want to be a rodeo clown, buy a big red nose, some shiny pants, and get out there and make some bulls look at you.

In 1996, Dave Kerpen was a college student selling concessions at Boston sporting events. Concession sales is a commissioned gig- -if you don't sell, you don't eat, and since Dave was the low man on the totem pole, he was assigned the arena's worst seller: Crunch 'n Munch.

On his first night out he sold 12 boxes and made the minimum commission $15.

Before going back for his second night's work, he decided that getting into the games for free and pocketing $15 wasn't good enough. He needed to make a living at this, so he had to step up his game. When he showed up in the stands for his encore performance, he made it just that, a performance. He sang a little, danced a little, cracked a few jokes, screamed, shouted and hammed it up good.

That night he sold three times as many boxes of sweet and salty goodness.

And now that he had a plan, he ramped the schtick up even farther, catching the eye of the arena cameraman, and The Crunch 'n Munch Guy was born. Soon, he didn't need to march through the stands hawking snacks. The crowd came to him, stood in line for AUTOGRAPHED boxes from the Crunch 'n Munch guy, and sent him back to his dorm room with $500 a night.

Kerpen is the first to admit he had no discernable talent--can't sing, can't dance. But what he did have was the willingness to take a chance, to take a leap of faith. The willingness to put himself out there.

Because bashful salespeople have skinny children.

Once he decided he was an entertainer and celebrity …

Once he acted AS IF he were an entertainer and celebrity …

Then that's exactly how the crowds treated him.

And he was rewarded by that standard.

Nobody cares what you say you are, what you say you're going to do.

People care about what you do, the actions that you take, the decisions that you make.

Quit talking about it and do something about it.

Act AS IF you are already everything you want to someday be.

Act AS IF you're leading the life you were born to lead.

Positive thinking can make you feel better, but positive acting is what makes shit happen.

ACTION STEPS

1) JOIN TinyHabits.com. B.J. Fogg regularly conducts week-long programs that let you choose your own three tiny habits to work on with daily email interaction and encouragement from him and his staff.

AFTER I

_____,

I will

_____.

AFTER I

_____,

I will

_____.

AFTER I

_____,

I will

_____.

2) SMILE. We have an expression in Tennessee--Shit Eating Grin. I've never really understood what that means or why that would be something to smile about, but everyone around here knows what it is: just a big ol' cheesy grin, the kind that makes your face hurt, like you've been eating fruit loops and watching a Scooby Doo marathon, ear to ear, baby, let's see it.

3) PUT ONE THING AWAY. Take a look around you and find one thing out of place, a shoe that never made it to the closet, a glass that never made it back to the kitchen. Take 20 seconds, right now, and put one thing back where it belongs.

4) GET RID OF ONE THING. This is harder. Take a look around, find one thing you've been hanging onto for far too long and toss that sucker. Trash it. Recycle it. Give it away. I don't care what you do with it, just get it out of your life.

5) GIVE THANKS. Close your eyes and say a quick prayer of thanks. Thank God. Thank the Eight Pound Six Ounce Tiny Baby Jesus. Thank Allah. Thank the Giant Turtle That Holds the Universe on Its Back. Thank whatever you believe in. Something greater than you has given you this amazing life. Even if you believe it was all random happenstance, it's just good manners to say thanks.

6) MAKE A BUSINESS CALL. Pick up the phone, right now and call an old customer you haven't spoken with in a while, a new prospect you've been meaning to call, a business associate that you need to reconnect with, your boss, an employee, anyone, pick up the phone and make something happen.

7) DROP AND GIVE ME ONE. One pushup, right here and now. You don't even have to wait till you go pee!

8) MAKE A TO DO LIST. Not a wish list. Not a mission statement. not a vision board. Take a minute or two and write down some things that you can do today to make your life better. Things you can do without buying any new equipment, without spending money, without coming up with a 17-point plan. Now do those things.

9) TIP OUTLANDISHLY. Tonight at dinner. Tomorrow at lunch. At the salon getting your nails done. The next time you leave a tip, leave a big one, twice as much as you normally do. Being generous feels good. Try it.

10) DO THE HAPPY DANCE. Celebrating your victories is the hard part for many people. Get over it. You've made it this far. Stand up, put your arms in the air, shake your moneymaker, and repeat after me: "Winner Winner Chicken Dinner."

For more info on the amazing transformative power of action, visit TerryLancaster.com/TakeAction.

Today Is The Day The Lord Has Made. Rejoice And Be Glad In It.

3. Be Grateful

Expectations Are The Enemy Of Happiness,
But Gratitude Is Its BFF.

Your life will never be BETTER, until you're able to acknowledge just how GOOD it really is right now.

In Chapter 1 we talked about the problem with perfection: How skipping right past BETTER and aiming for BEST is a recipe for failure. How people don't usually go from living in a van down by the river to a mansion on the hill overnight. We all want to go from worst to first:

BAD ⇨ BEST

But you're not really in a van down by the river, are you? I suspect you're in a nice, modest home probably about twice the size of the home you grew up in.

In this chapter, I want to talk about readjusting our sights in the other direction. We don't have to make the gigantic, insurmountable leap from BAD to BEST. Our lives aren't anywhere near as BAD as we make them out to be in our heads. In fact, they're not bad at all. They're pretty damn GOOD.

And the truth is who needs a mansion on the hill anyway? Just think about all the headache and upkeep! Forgetaboutit. This book is about real people making their real lives better. I'm never gonna be George Clooney. Hell, I'm barely George Costanza. But I'm not trying to be either one. All I want is to be a BETTER Terry Lancaster.

Since our lives aren't all that BAD and BEST isn't the goal anymore, we only have to get from GOOD to BETTER.

We're halfway there before we even get started!

BAD ⇨ *GOOD* ⇨ ***BETTER*** ⇨ BEST

You've got troubles. I've got troubles. We've all got troubles.

Traffic sucks and working for a living is not as much fun as it sounds like. Your kids are annoying and your dog smells funny ... or is it the other way around?

My biggest complaint in life right now is I can't get a Wi-Fi connection on one of the 3 Wi-Fi-enabled DVRs in my home ... woe is me.

No matter how bad we think we have it, though, I'd be willing to bet that 99% of the people who ever walked the face of the earth would trade places with you in a New York minute.

We've all got it pretty good and that ain't bad!

But most of the time, we don't think about how good we have it. It's much easier to bitch and moan about what isn't going our way.

In many respects, our brain is hardwired to pay attention to the negative. For ancient humans stopping to smell the roses was a dangerous pastime. There were lions and tigers and bears to worry about. Positive thinking could get you killed. Oh My.

So we get into the habit of thinking about what's wrong in our lives instead of what's right. And your brain is like a well worn dirt road. Once your negative thoughts start building ruts, that's the path you naturally take … bitching and moaning about how shitty your life is, mostly out of habit.

Our brain is only capable of processing a tiny, tiny fraction of all the information that we are bombarded with every day, so it takes short cuts. It only processes information that it thinks might be relevant.

In much the same way that Google decides which search results to show you and Facebook decides which one of your friends' cats you're going to see on your news feed, your brain uses an algorithm of sorts to decide which information makes it past the filter. Which reality makes the cut.

Your brain takes what's on your mind, and that's what it notices from the real world. It's called confirmation bias.

If you just dropped 30 grand on a shiny new red car, you're going to have shiny new red cars on the brain, and your brain is going to notice all the shiny new red cars on the road.

We see what we expect to see.

And if you spend all day thinking about how miserable your life is, your brain is going to find the data points it needs to confirm your bias. The traffic will suck more. Your boss will be a bigger asshole. Your kids will be even more annoying and your dog will smell even funnier.

But you can get your mind out of the ruts you've dug for yourself.

Everyday spend a little more time being thankful for what's going right in your life and a little less time thinking about what's going wrong.

When gratitude becomes a habit, you'll start to notice all that you have to be thankful for. When you're thankful for a chance to work and support your family, your boss will seem like less of an asshole. When you're thankful for the love and joy your children bring into your life, they won't seem quite as annoying.

Your dog will probably still smell funny, but when you're as excited to see him at the end of the day as he is to see you, you probably won't even notice.

Happiness is like a hagfish.

Yes, I know that may be the silliest sentence ever written. But stay with me here.

The hagfish is some kind of prehistoric looking fishy, eely kind of thingy that has developed a unique defense mechanism: whenever anything grabs or bites down on a hagfish, it releases massive amounts of slime from every pore in its body. In the wild that serves to clog the gills of predators who quickly lose interest in lunch.

For humans, grabbing a hagfish is much like trying to grab a handful of snot. And the harder you grasp, the snottier it gets.

Ironically, happiness works in much the same way.

The more you grab and grasp and lunge at happiness, the more difficult it is to obtain. The harder you pursue it, the farther away it becomes.

Philosophers have a name for this. It's called the Paradox of Pleasure.

The moment you ask yourself if you're happy is the moment you cease to be.

For the last 30 years or so, the whole world has sang along with Bobby McFerrin's "Don't Worry Be Happy," the feel good song of the century.

But telling yourself to be happy is like me telling my 5' 6" self to be taller. Believe me; I've tried. It doesn't work.

There are lots of things you can do to make yourself happier, but trying to be happy isn't one of them.

And too often our desperate pursuit of happiness becomes a pursuit of fun or pleasure, which aren't really the same as happiness at all. Hence the paradox.

Happiness is a side effect, and you can no more grab a handful of it than you can grab a handful of air, water, or hagfish.

But unlike air, water, and the prehistoric hagfish, happiness has a handle that you CAN grab onto. It's called gratitude.

The surest path to happiness is spending more time being grateful for what's right in your life and less time worrying about what's wrong.

What would make you happier--Winning a couple hundred million dollars in the next Powerball drawing, or being involved in an accident that resulted in you being confined to a wheelchair for life?

Well that's a silly question, right? I'm sure everyone would agree that winning the lottery would provide us with infinitely more happiness than becoming a paraplegic.

And it turns out that everyone is wrong.

According to research from Harvard psychologist Dan Gilbert, one year after their trauma, paraplegics are equally as happy as people who won the lottery a year earlier.

Dramatic life events, the powerful stuff of our hopes and dreams and worries and fears, have little to no effect on our happiness after just 3 months passage of time.

Abraham Lincoln was right. *"Most folks are about as happy as they make up their minds to be."*

Most of us are waiting for our real lives to start. Hinging our hopes for happiness on some future something. Everything will be OK if I can just (meet someone, lose weight, get a raise/promotion). Or even worse, we delay happiness because of fear or worry about what might happen if we (lose our job, have an accident, get sick).

We let an imaginary there and then screw up a perfectly good here and now.

When the truth is, scientists and philosophers have shown over and over again that happiness is not dependent upon, correlated with or caused by external factors.

Happiness is an internal function and we manufacture it in our heads.

Your brain can be a happiness factory or a misery factory, and which one it becomes is entirely and completely up to you.

The mind is its own place and in itself, can make a Heaven of Hell, a Hell of Heaven." --John Milton

The problem is, our brain lies to us. It tells us all the things that we think will make us happy, so we chase happiness around the world fighting wars, leaving spouses, buying more stuff, quitting good jobs. And happiness remains ever just outside our reach.

But the happiness we seek is within us all along, if we'd just quit looking so damn hard.

We manufacture happiness in our brain by taking away the if and the when.

Quit telling yourself: *I'll be happy if …*

Quit telling yourself: *I'll be happy when …*

And just tell yourself: *I am happy.*

Just like magic! ABRACADABRA.

We all know that favorite word of mustachioed magicians everywhere. What many of you may not know is that *abracadabra* is derived from the ancient Aramaic words avra kehdabra meaning *"I create as I speak."*

If you want to be happy, say you are happy. Act happy. Be happy.

Don't squander the countless blessings you have seeking ones you don't.

The stuff you have now is fine. The life you have now is amazing. You, my friend are a bona fide miracle. Eternity and all the forces in the universe have conspired to bring you to exactly this place and this time. This here and this now.

"There are only two ways to live your life. One is as if nothing is a miracle. The other is as if everything is." --Albert Einstein

I think Ol' Uncle Al may have been understating the obvious.

Anyone who has decided that there's no such thing as miracles just isn't paying attention.

Right now, while you sit here sipping your coffee, possibly reading these words on a device that holds the sum total of all human knowledge, you are spinning, along with everything else on the planet, at over 1,000 miles per hour. And we act like it's just another Tuesday afternoon. We're not flying off into space screaming at the top of our lungs. We haven't even spilled our Venti Half-Caf Double Mocha Latte.

1,000 miles an hour, though, is nothing more than a rounding error on our true rate of travel. We're circling the sun, even as we speak, at more than 66,000 miles an hour.

And that's STILL just barely a rounding error.

When I was a kid, back when Pluto was still a planet, I made a model of the solar system out of plywood and a few Styrofoam balls covered in Day-Glo paint (plus cardboard rings for Saturn). Pluto wasn't the only thing I got wrong, though.

We think of the planets travelling around the Sun in a never ending loop, kinda like one big Sunday afternoon NASCAR race. But that's not entirely accurate. We're not circling around the sun so much as we're chasing after it.

The sun isn't just sitting there like some giant tetherball pole. It's circling around the center of the Milky Way Galaxy.

And the Milky Way Galaxy itself is travelling at mind boggling speeds through the universe.

All told, while you sit here sipping your coffee, chatting and reading, you're traveling at a speed of close to 2 million miles per hour. You're hundreds of thousands of miles from where you were just minutes ago when you started reading this chapter.

And you'll never be back there again.

Gravity is the miraculous force that keeps us anchored to the floor of our 2 million mile per hour rocket ship. But gravity is the weakest force in the universe. And that's what leaves room for another miracle.

The miracle of stuff.

All the stuff you see around you right now, all the stuff you can touch and feel, well here's a surprise for you: There's nothing there. Technically, there's MOSTLY nothing there. They taught you in grade school science that all that stuff is made up of atoms, but atoms are mostly nothing.

If you were to blow a typical atom up to the size of the Earth, the proton at the center would be about the size of a basketball. A handful of electrons, which are thousands of times smaller, would be scattered around the planet. And the rest? Crickets. Nothing.

There's no there, there

The chair you're sitting on is made out of nothing. The only reason you don't crash onto the floor of Starbucks, the only reason stuff seems like stuff, is because the forces holding the atoms together are millions of times stronger than gravity. What you call stuff, is basically a force field. Really.

The miracle of you.

You're only here today because 1,000 generations ago, when your ancestor was being chased by a saber-toothed tiger, he was slightly faster than the other guy he was running with. If your great great great great-grandfather had asked the little redheaded girl to dance at the barn raising instead of the little blonde headed girl, there would be no you.

Miracles happened at every step, every day, every generation, to create the unique you.

You started out in this world as a single sperm cell racing in a marathon to glory against a couple of hundred million of your closest friends.

And you won!

Winner Winner. Chicken Dinner.

Winning that race created the unique DNA sequence that created you. If you were somehow able to translate your DNA sequence into words it would take three billion of them.

Three billion words to describe the Miracle of You. Reading your genome, describing yourself out loud, would take over a century.

And then there's the biggest completely unexplainable miracle of them all:

The miracle of now.

All around us everything we see, feel, touch, smell, think, or imagine exists as tiny bundles of light, particles of energy popping into and out of existence trillions of time a second, suspended in a constant state of indefinity, neither here nor there, neither now nor then, a slurry of possibility, everything that ever was or will be, everything that ever could be or could have been all dancing together side by side until somehow, by force of some scientifically inexplicable cosmic magic trick our being, our essence, our consciousness lights upon this kaleidoscope of the gods and collapses infinity into this brief shining miracle we call Now.

And then another.

And then another.

Seems like the least we can do is say thanks.

The point is we are surrounded by miracles. The miracle of gravity. The miracle of stuff that's made out of stuff that isn't really stuff at all. The miracle of simply being HERE in the first place.

We're only here for the blink of an eye. And the best way, probably the only way, to find true happiness in this life is to appreciate it for the miracle it is.

But appreciating what you have is a difficult proposition, because there's always someone who has more stuff. There's always someone who has better stuff.

Faster Cars. Bigger Houses. Better Behaved, More Attractive Children.

Their kids make the AAA Travel Pee Wee Hockey team and your kids barely made the AA team.

They get to travel to exotic locations for work and pleasure and you get to go to the 10 o'clock Monday morning Workplace Procedures and Protocols meeting for the 173rd Monday morning in a row.

Life has always been unfair.

There's always been the haves and the have nots.

The problem now is our non-stop, 24 hour a day feedback loop that shows us in never ending detail just how much the haves have.

Whether we're Keeping up with the Kardashians on TV or keeping up with the Jones's on Facebook, our lives pale in comparison.

Psychology Today says that a full one third of Facebook users are unhappier after stalking their friends on Facebook, because real life is a dull substitute for the never ending stream of promotions, new kids, and exciting vacations we see on our friends' newsfeeds.

And then there's porn.

Late the other night, home alone, the lights off in the house, I was curled up on the couch flipping channels and "accidentally" found myself intensely watching … a late night TV preacher.

Not where you thought I was going, huh?

This wasn't your stereotypical hellfire and brimstone, cheap polyester suit Bible thumper. He was a young preacher with blue jeans and a PowerPoint talking about the neurological reasons that pornography makes you unhappy.

Porn hardwires a man's brain for dissatisfaction, because no real live woman can ever compete with an infinite supply of never aging, super-sexual porn stars who never have bad hair days and never nag us to take out the trash.

Porn is simply another way of letting an imaginary there and then screw up a perfectly good here and now.

But that isn't the problem with porn.

The problem with porn is that we've let our need for immediate gratification, for wanting to have it all (and if we can't have it all then for at least getting to look at it all) invade almost every area of our lives.

There are entire industries devoted to feeding us visual stimulation and helping us part ways with our money.

House Porn with Vanilla Ice installing silky smooth new granite countertops and hardwood floors just like momma likes.

Car Porn with purring engines, dangerous curves, and pumping pistons that get daddy all revved up.

Wiping peanut butter and jelly stains off your Formica countertops and driving to work in your nine-year-old Chevy just doesn't get the job done after watching that.

Because comparisons make us unhappy.

That's one reason why I've always been dubious of The Secret and

Law of Attraction aficionados who tell us to intensely imagine all the things we ever wanted and they will manifest into our lives. They have dream boards filled with collages of beautiful homes, exotic sports cars, gold jewelry, 100-foot yachts, and great big stacks of cold hard cash. And maybe if you concentrate hard enough, all of that stuff will just magically appear.

But if you spend all day staring at a dream board full of stuff you don't have, you've got a lot less time to be grateful for all the awesome stuff that you do have.

Porn, in all it forms, is an expression of ingratitude: "I like this shiny stuff better than my real stuff. Why, oh why, can't I have nice stuff too?"

So here's my version of THE SECRET:

Build yourself a dream board filled with pictures of all the amazing things that exist in your real life: The spouse who still loves you despite knowing what your morning breath smells like. The perfectly good home you live in now that gives you and your family a place to live, shelter from the storm. The nine-year-old Chevy that gets you anywhere you want to go.

Just a few hundred years ago any king in the world would have given up half his possessions for your three-bedroom ranch and nine-year-old Chevy. And the vast majority of people walking the face of the earth today still would.

Instead of dreaming about what could be, be more grateful for what is. Rejoice in the way things are and try every day to make them just a little bit better.

That's The Real Secret.

My life started to turn around when I put away the dream board, quit listening to the Don Lapres and Matt Foleys of the world, and started listening to 90s pop sensation--The Spice Girls.

Tell Me What You Want, What You Really, Really Want ...

When I was a young man, fresh out of college, I had a three-foot wide poster of a Porsche 911 Turbo hanging on my office wall-- Black on Black, with the flared fenders and the whale tail. In my 24-year-old mind, that Porsche was what I really, really wanted. It was the reason I got up and went to work every morning.

It was #1 on my lottery list.

We've all got one, right? The list of things we're going to buy when we win the lottery. And I've read enough self help and motivational books over the years that I've answered the big WHAT IF hundreds of times. WHAT would you do IF money were no object. And as a younger man, obviously, if money were no object, I'd have bought a shit load of stuff starting with a black on black 911 Porsche Turbo. Duh!

But life has a funny way of changing your priorities. After you get kicked in the sack by life's up and downs enough times, after the golden ring gets dangled in front of your nose and jerked away enough times, after you come to grips with your mortality enough times, maybe, if you're lucky, your priorities change.

One day while sitting in my backyard on my deck drinking coffee playing the WHAT IF game, it occurred to me that WHAT I REALLY, REALLY WANT-ed, what I had always REALLY, REALLY WANT-ed wasn't the black on black 911 Turbo.

I didn't REALLY, REALLY care about buying a major league sports team, or building a skyscraper with my name on it. I didn't want a 100-foot-yacht on the Mediterranean or a Penthouse in New York. All of those things were too far removed from my real life to have any meaning.

I didn't want the lifestyles of the rich and famous. WHAT I REALLY, REALLY WANTED was my actual life, the life I was already living, ONLY BETTER.

I wanted the job I already had ONLY BETTER.

I wanted the home I already lived in ONLY BETTER.

I wanted the marriage I already had ONLY BETTER.

It occurred to me that maybe If I quit playing WHAT IF about all the amazing stuff I could have if the stars were to align themselves properly, I could concentrate on FIXING the amazing stuff that I already had.

I didn't need to burn everything down and start all over again.

I needed to be a better steward to the blessings that I had already been given.

You'll never get where you're going unless you start where you are.

It turns out that all that green, green grass on the other side of the fence …

It's still just grass.

The same as yours.

Sometimes it's greener. Sometimes it's not. But it doesn't matter.

What matters is the grass on your side of the fence.

When you learn to appreciate the grass you already have, to be truly grateful for it, to water it and nurture it and tend it and enjoy it, you'll probably find the same thing I did.

Your side of the fence is all that really matters.

ACTION STEPS

1) COUNT YOUR BLESSINGS. Let's make a list, a list of everything that's right in your life. A list of things that bring you happiness. A List of things that bring you peace. A list of things that make you smile. A list of things that have happened in your life to bring you to where you are. And while we're at, let's list all the things that make you who you are. What is it about you that makes you most proud? Who brings joy into your life. Who can you count on when the chips are down. When the shit hits the fan, who are you calling for bail money and a shovel? Whether you know it or not, you've been blessed beyond your wildest imagination. It's time to take inventory. This could take a while. We'll wait.

2) SAY THANK YOU. We all learned to say please and thank you in kindergarten, but somewhere along the way we forgot. We're taught to say thanks because it's the polite thing to do and because it makes the other person feel appreciated and that's all well and good, but you need to do it mostly for you. Thinking grateful thoughts fires one set of neurons in your head. Writing thank you notes fires another. Saying grateful things out loud fires yet another, and the big idea is to make as many gratitude neural connections in your brain as possible so that it becomes a well worn highway. Send thank you notes to some of the people you listed in Step 1. pick up the phone and call some others. Say thank you and let them know how they've made your life better.

3) SIT, BREATHE AND BE THANKFUL. Take 10 or 15 minutes today to go outside, sit in the sunshine, breathe in the fresh air, and just be thankful. Don't think of things to be thankful for. Just feel grateful. And Smile.

4) DAILY INVENTORY. Today, at the end of the day, take a moment to reflect on all the good things that happened. Waking up above ground is a good place to start.

5) TAKE A VACATION. Let's start with a week. Seven days, seven nights without bitching, moaning, complaining, or whining. When you feel negative thoughts creeping in, just tell your head to SHUT

UP and find something in that situation to be grateful for instead.

6) THE GRATITUDE CHALLENGE. Ancient people expressed their intentions to the universe by climbing a mountain and chanting; today we just go to Facebook. So head on over to Facebook, right now and tell the universe (or at least your 483 closest friends) three things that you're grateful for. See how many days in a row you can do that.

For more info on how to create happiness through gratitude visit TerryLancaster.com/gratitude.

TERRY LANCASTER

Real Food. Clean Water. Fresh Air And Sunshine.
Everything Else Is optional.

4. Fuel The Machine

—

Get the Fuel You Need For The Life You Lead.

—

I wish I could say that the 300 pounds I weighed a few years ago was the heaviest I've ever been, but it's not. This ain't my first rodeo. I've hit the big 3-0-0 before, lost it, and then gained the vast majority of it back over time for the exact same reasons that everyone else does.

Diets don't work. Period.

I've been on Nutrisystem, Atkins, South Beach, Shangri La, and my all time favorite, the See Food Diet; I've been on that one a lot!

It's actually fairly easy to lose weight on a diet. On almost any diet … Five, 10, even 20 percent of your body weight. Only to regain it as soon as you slip back into "maintenance" mode.

But that's not my definition of success. I'm weary of the restart button.

These diet companies spend billions on advertising, because there's BIG money in making you feel bad about yourself and then selling you shit to ease the pain.

Their ads are all about the Before and After photo. Fat to Fit. Zero to Hero.

Bad ⇨ Best

But we're just trying to get BETTER!

Success is MAINTAINING a healthy weight, and for that diets are miserable failures.

But we all know that.

We know the basic psychology: denying that which you crave, only makes you crave it more.

We know that starving your body sends it into starvation mode. Your brain plays defense by slowing down your metabolism and offense by pumping out hormones that make you seek out even more food.

We know that cutting calories eats into lean muscle tissue, denying us the ability to burn off the few calories that we do eat.

It's a vicious cycle perpetrated by a multi-billion dollar diet industry and the built in human desire for easy answers.

It sounds great. If we can only build up the willpower, we can "diet" for a few months, eat nothing but grapefruit seeds and black coffee, lose those love handles, and our whole lives will magically turn around.

The unspoken premise is that once we've lost the weight, we can go back to normal. Normal being our regular Big Mac and Cheesecake Diet. Deep down, we know that's a lie, but we'll worry about that after we lose the weight.

Of course we gain it all back. And more because we've screwed up our metabolism, destroyed our muscles, and wreaked havoc on our fragile psychology. So we eat more to numb the pain. And the cycle starts all over again.

Cause here's the thing.

You can't change your life without changing your lifestyle.

Diets are a Band-Aid, and we need a whole new way of living.

A whole new way of feeding the machine that is us.

We have to distinguish the food that we want from the fuel that we need.

And we really only need four things to make the machine run:

Real Food. Clean Water. Fresh Air and Sunshine.

Everything is else is optional.

There's growing evidence that the obesity epidemic in America, which is either a cause or a symptom of many chronic conditions, is not simply a result of the fact that we eat too much and exercise too little, but also because we eat the wrong food.

Or to be precise, because we mostly don't eat food. We eat pre-packaged edible food-like products with little to no nutritional value. They take out all the nutrition, package it in shiny boxes, and then sell us multi-vitamins to make up the difference. More pills.

What passes for food in America is actually a delivery system to feed our sugar addiction. Sugar is America's true drug of choice.

Between sugar overload and the residual chemicals and antibiotics from processing and packaging, what we eat overloads the bacterial population of our digestive tract, altering the way we metabolize sugars, store fat, and respond to hormonal signals that tell us when we're full.

Losing weight isn't like quitting smoking or drinking or heroin or anything else, we say. People can quit smoking cold turkey. You can stop drinking and never have to touch another glass of alcohol. Once you're off the needle, you're off the needle.

You don't HAVE to smoke, drink, or sniff glue, but food, that's different we say. "I'm addicted to food. I HAVE to eat."

Well, that's bullshit and here's why.

It's actually quite amazing how little food the human body needs. You can live for weeks and weeks without any food at all. Some people have lived for years on 1000-1500 calories a day, claiming that extreme calorie restriction can actually increase your lifespan.

We need food. We need to eat to live. But we don't actually NEED anywhere close to the amount of food we eat.

I've been experimenting a little lately with intermittent fasting which is just a fancy way of saying eating at controlled intervals. One or two days a week, I'll only eat around 600 calories. Then on other days, I eat regularly.

The biggest benefit has been to see actually how little food I need to function normally.

That and to see what actual hunger feels like. If you only eat 200 calories in the morning, by afternoon, you're actually hungry which is an entirely different sensation than WANTING something to eat.

Mainly because when we WANT something to eat, it usually isn't food.

It's just sugar in myriad disguises.

We may not be able to give up food completely the way other addicts go cold turkey, but if we can start to recognize our true addiction, we can start to separate what we want from what we need.

Food isn't the problem. Sugar is the problem.

Americans love sugar more than a fat kid loves cake ... actually pretty much exactly the same as a fat kid loves cake.

Which is to say ... a whole, whole lot.

We eat about 100 pounds of sugar each and every year.

When Hostess filed for bankruptcy, we went into a national state of crisis over the impending lack of Twinkies. We were buying them up on eBay for a thousand bucks a box and hoarding them in the attic like the zombies were coming for our Twinkies instead of our brains.

Truth is, it's our brains that are the zombies ... zombies for sugar.

And it's not just the sugar in the fat kid's cakes and candy bars. We're addicted to sugar in all its forms. All the junk foods. All the fast foods. All the foods that aren't really foods, because they contain almost no nutritional value, just empty calories ... and sugar.

Sugar is a glorious thing. It makes your brain sparkle.

But sugar isn't a food. It's a drug.

Food fuels you, nourishes you, strengthens you, gives you the energy you need to lead your life.

Sugar just tastes oh so sweet and scratches an itch in your head. But like heroin, or nicotine, or booze it provides no lasting sustenance or relief.

Only the desire, the need to scratch the itch again. And soon.

Hell, it says so on the package: no one can eat just one.

We're addicted to sugar and its horde of carbohydrate carriers. We're no more likely to put down an open bag of cookies than a crackhead is to put down the pipe.

But the first step to overcoming any addiction is admitting that there is a problem.

Food isn't why you're fat. Food isn't the problem.

Sugar is the problem.

Yes, we have to eat, but if we can make the switch from eating for fun to eating for fuel, from eating because it tastes good to eating because it is good, from eating out of habit to eating because we're hungry--if we can do that, we'll eat less.

How do we do that? By eating real food.

I was driving home one night from an after-work function, around eight o'clock or so, and I was starving. Not starving in the third world country sense of the word, but starving in a middle-aged, chubby suburban kind of way. I hadn't eaten since lunchtime and I was seriously ready for a big mac, a quarter pounder, chocolate shake, and, yes, I would like fries with that.

The entire $120 billion fast food industry has been built on moments just like those. I was in my car, pre-occupied with food. Too tired to cook and too hungry to wait. I was looking for the nearest exit with golden arches when a momentary fit of self discipline kicked in.

I have a little spreadsheet I keep on my desk of things I'd like to accomplish every day and one of them is EAT 3 VEGETABLES. I would have been perfectly willing to drive-thru for a Fast Food Fix, but I hadn't filled my quota of veggies for the day--time for Plan B.

Plan B was to stop for take out at Pei Wei Asian Diner. Pei Wei attempts to fill the gap between fine dining and fast food. Kind a good food fast concept, and it's not bad. One of my favorite "healthy" meals is a trip to Pei Wei for a quick take home meal, but instead of the usual pile of rice and noodles, I'll have them hold the starch and load up the plate with extra veggies and protein, then make it extra spicy for a little added metabolism boost.

Of course the sauce is still loaded with sugar, so it's not like I'm eating off the weight watchers menu, but it's not fast food and I get to punch my vegetables card for that day.

A trip to Pei Wei costs 2 or 3 times what a run for the border costs. But it's almost as fast and, hey, at least it's real food.

So I'm off the interstate, driving past the Golden Arches and on my way to Pei Wei, planning my order in my head. When Plan C hits me.

Sitting at home in my fridge, I've got a week old bag of broccoli, some leftover chicken, some salad greens, carrots, snap peas and onion that are all on the verge of being tossed in the garbage.

Between leftovers and food we never got around to actually cooking in the first place, Americans, especially busy, chubby, suburban Americans, throw away almost as much food as we actually eat.

So plan C was leftovers. Because Veggies.

And instead of dropping $10-$15 bucks on take out, I get to eat for free, because otherwise it all gets tossed. Everybody likes free.

But there's still the question of time. I'm still starving, I still don't have the time or the willpower to cook. I still want food and I still want it fast.

So here's my super secret hot tip of the day:

If you want to

save time on meal preparation

save money by using leftovers

save the planet by throwing away less food

eat healthier by eating more vegetables and proteins

and lose weight by cutting the starch and sugars out of your meals …

Buy a Wok.

I got home, threw the wok on the stove to heat up, splashed in a little oil and then opened the fridge for leftover heaven.

Broccoli, Carrots, Snow Peas, Onions, Red Bell Pepper, some salad greens, a couple of pieces of cold chicken, a dash of soy sauce and a good 2 or 3 dashes of my old stand by, Frank's Hot Sauce, and BAM!!! 10 minutes from the time I hit the door, I was dipping my chopsticks into some primo Chicken à la Terry.

I didn't cost me a dime that wasn't already spent. It was quick enough that I resisted Ray Kroc's siren song on a sesame seed bun. And best of all … It was good eating.

The news people love to talk about how expensive real food is, and sure, it costs a little more than the 99¢ value menu, but it's REAL FOOD.

You can just about fill up the crisper with fresh veggies for what a single meal at the nearby good food fast joint costs.

That and my handy, dandy, well-oiled, well-seasoned wok will keep my belly full all week long.

And I get to punch the veggie card every day!

Every diet book in the history of diet books encourages you to drink more water.

It's filling and it's calorie free. Plus if you get in the habit of drinking water, you're more likely to break the habit of drinking all the other crap that's killing you--soda, sports drinks, and booze--which are all either loaded to the brim with sugar (alcohol is sugar!) or worse yet with artificial sweeteners that screw with your metabolism and satiety response.

Being even slightly dehydrated can sap your energy and keep you on the couch instead of up and moving getting the exercise your body dearly needs.

Water flushes your body of toxins, allowing your immune system to stand down from its constant state of emergency, improving your digestive and metabolic functions so you need, that's right, fewer pills!

Some research shows that people who drink five glasses of water a day cut their risk of a heart attack by 40% over those who only drink two glasses a day.

Drink Up, Buttercup!

Eat on purpose and on schedule.

Your grandmother probably told you not to eat late at night because you didn't burn off as many calories and it made you fat.

Today, nutritionists disagree on whether late night eating in and of itself can cause weight gain, but recent studies at Northwestern University show that mice that ate when they should have been sleeping gain weight twice as fast as mice that at on a more natural schedule.

As much as 85% of our Human Growth Hormone (HGH), which aids in metabolic function, tissue growth and muscle repair, is produced at night during deep cycle sleep. Late night snacking, especially on carbohydrates, can create insulin spikes, limiting the production of HGH and leading to fatigue, slower recovery times, and weight gain.

Nutritionists all agree, though, that late night eating can cause insomnia, indigestion, acid reflux, AND weight gain if you're consuming more calories than needed in the form of calorie dense carbohydrates. And let's face it, nobody's sitting in front of the tube all night stuffing their face with broccoli and kale. It's ice cream and Doritos, baby. All night long.

I've been a night owl since before I even knew what a night owl was. Late night snacking was a major factor in my weight creeping up into the 300 pound neighborhood. It wasn't unusual for me to consume a third to half of my daily calorie intake AFTER dinner, sitting on the couch watching crappy TV 'til 3 in the morning.

For the first time in my life, though, I feel like I've gotten a handle on the late night munchies. Here's how:

Eat for fuel.

The first hurdle, and the hardest, is convincing yourself to eat for fuel. Not for fun. Not out of habit. Not because it tastes good. Eat to provide your body with the fuel it needs.

When you find yourself in front of the fridge trying to figure out what you want, understand that you're not there because you're hungry. You don't need much fuel to sleep through the night, and ice cream and Doritos aren't exactly rocket fuel anyway.

You're there out of habit. You're there out of boredom. And you're there to satisfy your addiction to sugar.

Starting to think of food as fuel for the engine of your life is half the battle.

Brush your teeth.

Brush your teeth right after dinner. As you're standing in front of the fridge, your minty fresh breath will serve as a reminder to close the door. If you eat, you've just got to brush them all over again!

Drink more water.

Most of us are chronically dehydrated and it's easy to confuse hunger for thirst. Your body wants so your mind seeks. And once you actually get up and start seeking, that carton of Häagen Dazs looks like a pretty good choice.

One trick I use is to keep water bottles in the refrigerator door and every time I open the fridge, for any reason, I've got to drink at least half a bottle. Them's the rules.

Do something other than watch TV.

A lifetime of bad habits conditioned me to sit in front of the TV and eat crappy food. If this, then that. It's basic programming. I spent almost 50 years programming myself to be fat and lazy.

And then of course, there are the commercials. The junk food/fast food/packaged foods industrial complex spends billions on television advertising.

You wanna know why? Because it works.

The sole purpose of commercial TV is to make you feel dissatisfied and sell you shit to ease the pain.

Take a walk. Read a book. Clean the house. Talk to your family. Anything to keep the TV off for just a few more minutes.

And if you do have to watch the tube, use the DVR so that you can watch something you actually want to watch instead of wasting time surfing channels, desperately looking for something interesting, and then mistaking your mind-numbing boredom for hunger.

Eat real food.

Did you ever wonder why Cheetos are puffy? Because in addition to the billions Big Food spends on advertising, they spend billions more on research to determine exactly how to make you eat the most of their product without ever getting fully satisfied.

You call Cheetos puffy. The "food" scientists say that they have Vanishing Caloric Density. It turns out if something melts down in your mouth quickly, your brain assumes that it doesn't have any calories and you can eat it forever without getting full. That's just one of their tricks. If you just have to eat something late at night, eat real food. Protein from meat and vegetables. Fruit. Nuts. You're still consuming calories, but at least it's real food, fuel. Not some giant corporation's chemistry experiment.

And the best way to avoid all the junk food crap late at night? Don't bring it home from the store in the first place.

If it's not in the house, you can't eat it.

Eat mindfully.

If you do eat at night, or anytime really, you can dramatically cut down on the amount by being mindful of what you're eating.

The TV is the perfect distraction. While you're engrossed in that "Law and Order" rerun, your brain is barely even aware of the full carton of ice cream you just ate.

Be fully aware of what you're eating, why you're eating it, and how much of it you're eating.

Dish a single serving of Häagen Dazs, sit down at the table and savor it. If you're paying the caloric price, you might as well enjoy it instead of wolfing it down before you even realize it's gone. Taste the rainbow!

Relish your little transgression. Put everything back away. Wash the dishes. And brush your teeth, again!

Change the way you think about food. From eating for sport to eating for fuel. From eating out of habit to eating with purpose.

Treat sugar as a drug instead of a delicacy and definitely not as a staple.

You can create a better life by creating a better lifestyle--one that doesn't revolve around when and where and what you're going to eat. There are a couple of other things that your body needs to function at its highest level. And you can't get them at the grocery store.

Fresh air and sunshine.

There can't be too many things that are a bigger kick in the groin than a doctor saying the words "You have cancer."

Except for maybe a doctor letting you know that you have cancer without ever saying a word.

I had a mole on my stomach that had been growing for a couple of years, and to be honest, I just assumed it was because my stomach had also been growing for a couple of years. Then it started itching a little and I decided to go get it checked out, just to be on the safe side.

I really wasn't worried about it at all, but I had another mole on my face that I wanted removed purely out of vanity. I figured, two birds, one deductible. Why not?

So I'm sitting in the exam room, waiting on the dermatologist to come in and I pick up the brochure about skin cancer. It explains about the different kinds of skin cancer: the good kind, carcinoma, which can ruin your day, but is highly treatable. And the bad kind, melanoma, which is also highly treatable, IF it's found early before it spreads beyond the skin--metastasis.

The brochure described metastatic melanoma as one of the most invasive, deadliest cancers known to mankind. The Tyrannosaurus rex of cancer.

And the mole on my stomach which had been growing for years looked exactly like the melanoma pictured in the brochure. When the doctor walks in, I hand him the brochure, point to the picture and say "Doc, I've got one of these."

He actually chuckled, while he was washing his hands getting ready for the exam. He tells me that melanoma is extremely rare, especially in someone my age, and he wouldn't be too worried about and let's just take a little look see here …

And then he stopped chuckling.

The blood drained from his face, his pupils dilated and all the air got sucked out of the room.

The knot that formed in the pit of my stomach right then didn't loosen for for a decade.

Turns out that my melanoma hadn't spread yet, and all I've got to show for it now is a giant scar on my abdomen and the CD of music I made to play at my funeral after a particularly bad week when a misread X-ray had the doctors at Duke University convinced the melanoma had spread to my lungs.

The cancer hadn't spread, but the idea of the cancer took hold in my brain and set up camp. There probably wasn't a day that went by for five, maybe 10 years that I didn't think about having cancer.

Worrying about when it was going to show back up.

I was diagnosed when my youngest daughter was three months old. I had three children under the age of four.

Dying just wasn't an option. But worrying was. So I worried. And I did the only thing I thought I could do to keep the cancer from coming back. I stayed out of the sun.

Now the truth is, exposure to the sun isn't what puts you at risk for melanoma. It's OVER exposure to the sun, sunburns, that put you at risk. And even worse, tanning beds. But with the "I've got cancer" knot still in the pit of my stomach, all I heard was stay out of the sun. So that's what I did. Totally.

I was the palest white boy in the history of pale white boys.

And I was miserable.

Seasonal Affective Disorder (SAD) is a type of depression that typically occurs over the fall and winter months when people aren't exposed to enough sunlight.

I was SAD for a decade and a half.

Then a funny thing happened. I had started exercising a little, doing my own homegrown naked yoga/shadow boxing/tai chi/kinda, sorta regimen over the winter and, once it warmed for the summer, I took it outside.

Sunshine makes you happy.

I got into the habit most days at lunch of going outside, cleaning the pool, and doing my little workout. Outside. In the Sun. And it felt good.

Better than good actually, Unbelievable. Spiritual, even.

After I got over my initial fear of the sun, sometimes I would just stand there with the sun on my face, Enjoying the simple pleasure. The warm glow of now.

And I got my first tan since Bill Clinton was president.

Ancient cultures worshipped the sun for the warmth and energy it provided. For the crops it nourished. For the life it gave. But there was something more. It made them happy for reasons they didn't understand, so they worshipped the sun as a God.

Today, we know why.

Sunshine stimulates our body's production of melatonin, endorphins, and serotonin--hormones deeply entwined with our feelings of happiness, well-being, and satisfaction.

Sunlight even helps control your hunger.

With extra serotonin sparkling around your brain, you just feel more complete, more sated, and you have no need to go looking for Twinkies to scratch the itch in your head … the feeling you have when you just want something to eat, but you have no idea what it is. You can get thinner, happier, and tanner in one fell swoop.

Sunlight is truly a magic pill.

We get 90% to 95% of our body's vitamin D from sunshine. The Vitamin D we get from sunshine helps improve our immune system, decrease inflammation, including arthritis, lower our blood pressure and cholesterol, prevent cavities, and decrease our risk of heart disease and many forms of cancer.

Sunshine can even clear up acne, psoriasis, and eczema by sanitizing mold, bacteria, and viruses on your skin.

If the pharmaceutical industry could bottle sunshine and convince you that you had to have a prescription for it, there's no telling what they would charge.

OVER exposure is still deadly. Tanning beds are an evil abomination. Fake sun is just as bad as fake food. And I still find melanoma to be the scariest word in the English language, but I've come out of the shadows.

I'm happier. I'm thinner. I'm healthier.

And not nearly as pale.

Real Food. Clean Water. Fresh Air and Sunlight. That's all we really need to fuel the machine.

But we're living lifestyles that make us think we need a lot more. We've got a lot of monkeys on our backs, and we're putting a lot of other things in the tank.

And putting the wrong fuel in as just as bad for the machine as no fuel at all.

So I'm walking toward the door and my buddy's yelling at me from the bar.

"T, let me drive you home, dude. You can't drive. I've never seen you this drunk."

I scoff at him, drop my keys, stumble, pick them up and walk out the door. "Don't worry, bro. I got this."

He turns around and goes back to hitting on the (formerly, slightly attractive) meth addict sitting at the bar, and I get behind the wheel of my car.

It's 3 am on October 1, 2012. It's also my 48th birthday, and I proceed to drive home.

Or at least I assume I drove home because I honestly have no recollection after leaving the bar. For all I know I was abducted by aliens who took me home and parked my car crookedly in the driveway

They apparently also decided to clean my pool and then leave my blue jeans, along with my keys, wallet and cell phone, in a pile in the basement for an early morning game of hide and seek.

And by early morning, I mean the crack of 10. And by crack of 10, I mean almost 11.

All I know for sure is that when I woke up, I felt as if someone had driven a railroad spike into my skull, right between my eyeballs. Again.

Hank Williams, Jr. sang that "Hangovers hurt more than they used to." Truer words have never been spoken. I've been nursing hangovers since I was a teenager. I had it down to a science. But over the last few years they had gotten progressively worse and were regularly turning into two or even three day affairs.

So that morning I started doing what I always have done in that situation. I start negotiating and praying.

"Dear, sweet, tiny baby Jesus ..."

I swore I'd never drink again. And If I did accidently drink again, I'd only drink beer. No more Patron and Fireball shots for me. It's beer only from here on out. In fact, I'll only drink light beer, Coors Light, even. Hell that doesn't even count.

Of course, I didn't believe the words, even as I said them. I tried to rationalize why the night before "had gotten away from me." Maybe I hadn't eaten enough. I had lost a little weight and I was laying off the carbs--maybe that had affected the way my brain was processing the sugars in the alcohol.

Maybe I was just getting old.

I'd been drinking since I was 14 years old and prided myself on knowing my limits--being able to get just hammered enough to avoid serious consequences.

I had actually been attempting to moderate myself. But drinking less was just setting me up for failure by decreasing my tolerance and letting things "get away from me" more easily.

Then I had another epiphany.

When the drunk guy at the bar hitting on the meth addict becomes the voice of reason in your life, maybe it's time to reexamine your lifestyle.

So I decided to hit the reset button. Do a 31-day cleanse of sorts to get my head right, get my tolerance levels adjusted, and clear a path back to my standard binge drinking moderation.

I called it Sober October.

I spent the next month booze free, drinking only water at the bar after hockey games while all my buddies tipped them back. The hardest part was handing beers around the locker room after games. Nothing has ever tasted better than a frosty cold Canadian Lager after a hockey game.

But I abstained and a funny thing happened. I felt really good.

I lost a few pounds that month, gained a little energy, started walking regularly, and enjoyed 31 days without a hangover. I felt so good, I did it again in November.

By Christmas I had run a mile non-stop for the first time since I was in high school.

By Valentines Day I had run a 5K for the first time in my life.

I've been sober and hangover free for two and a half years.

That's the first time I can honestly say that since I was 14 years old.

And while I'm still a fat ass, I'm in the best shape I've ever been in, by a large margin. I've weighed a little less a couple of times, and maybe I was a little stronger when I was a younger man, but I wasn't healthy. And I've never felt better, functioned better or thought clearer.

Not being hungover three to four days out of the week makes all that possible.

I've always been a drinker, but I kidded myself into thinking I wasn't an alcoholic, because I didn't drink every day and because I had never suffered any MAJOR, DIRECT consequences from drinking. Sure I had banged up MY car once or twice. Sure I drank myself out of my college scholarship. But I'd never had a DUI, and I figured that meant I was doing OK, that I knew my limits.

I was actually half drunk when I took my driver's exam at 16. My mom surprised me by coming home from work early one day so I could go get my license, not knowing I had spent a couple of hours after school riding around East Nashville and drinking a six pack. I had a license to drive under the influence.

I wore my drinking man status like a badge of honor. Granddaddy was a drinking man. It's a family tradition (More Hank, there). And I can quote you statistics to prove that social drinkers are more successful, more creative, and make more money, not in spite of their drinking, but in part, because of it.

Most of my best friends, who am I kidding, all of my best friends, are highly functional, binge drinking alcoholics. Drinkers always find drinkers. And being sober hasn't stopped me from hanging out in bars with them, but it has saved me thousands of dollars over the last few years when the only drink on my tab has been water.

I never set out to quit drinking. I liked drinking. But I figured out I liked feeling good better.

And honestly, I didn't know how bad I had felt until I started feeling better.

Not just the hangovers, but the general run down feeling that had been tugging on me like an anchor for my entire life.

That's gone now.

You can't change your life without changing your lifestyle.

I told you in Chapter 2 that true success in almost any endeavor begins with being grateful for what you have.

I'm thankful for all the blessings in my life, and I'm not going to give it all up for a Big Mac and a Super Size Coke or another round of tequila shots.

ACTION STEPS

1) EAT A PEACH. Or a banana. Or an apple. Fruit is nature's candy, and it's REAL FOOD. I have a buddy who is a vegan bodybuilder (there's a couple of words your rarely see side by side) and he eats a dozen bananas a day. 30 pounds a week!

2) VEGGIES! VEGGIES! VEGGIES! You remember cooking, right? It happens in the kitchen. Oven? Stove? So tonight when you're cooking dinner using your favorite go to recipe whether it's spaghetti, Hamburger Helper, or tuna casserole, throw in a bag of mixed vegetables. I like Birdseye Steamfresh veggies. I'll nuke them for five minutes and then add them to my spaghetti sauce (sorry, gravy for my paisanos), whatever casserole I'm making, even scrambled eggs. Because Veggies!

3) CLEAN OUT YOUR PANTRY. Carb Patrol Time! If your house is anything like my house used to be, you have at least 17 varieties of cookies, crackers, breads, chips, etc. in the pantry. Toss 'em. If they're not in the house, you can't be tempted. And while you're in there, go ahead and toss about 90% of the rest of the crap you have in there out too. That can of Cream of Mushroom soup from 2003. The cake mix from that one time you were gonna try to be the Cake Boss. Get rid of all the pre-packaged, partially edible, food-like substances in there and make room for some real food.

5) DO A LAP AROUND THE GROCERY STORE. Walk into your neighborhood market and turn right. They put all the good, healthy stuff right there to trick you into believing everything they sell is real food. But they keep all the real food right there on the edge. Veggies. Fruits. Meats. Load up you cart with real food before you start getting to the stuff in boxes. Boxes bad.

6) TAKE A BIG DRINK OF WATER. Get yourself a nice big glass of cold water. If you can manage to not drink it out of a plastic bottle, that's even better. You know how the fast food commercial all have people making that nice big AHHHH noise every time they drink an ice cold soft drink (insert brand name here), water is every bit as refreshing. Your body really, really likes this stuff. Enjoy it. Savor it. Just say AHHH!

7) SOAK UP SOME RAYS. Go outside. Find a nice little sliver of sunlight. Point your face at it. And just sit there. Breathe in. Breathe out. Enjoy the warmth and bask in it. That little slice of heaven just travelled 93 million miles to warm your face.

8) A CUP OF JOE. I started drinking coffee at my grandfather's side when I was five years old, and for most of my life I drank it with equal parts, coffee, milk, and sugar. After I started trying to drink fewer calories, I weaned myself off the milk and sugar and started drinking my coffee black. The funny thing is, I discovered that the bitterness of black coffee acts like a switch shutting off the receptors that crave sweetness. Sipping on black coffee all day helps you want less sweetness and provides the best answer to the sugar vs. diet sweetener conundrum. The best answer is neither!

9) ONE WEEK. Maybe booze isn't the problem for you that it was for me. Maybe you're better at knowing when to say when. Odds are pretty good you are, but you know alcohol has powerful effects on your body and your mind--otherwise you wouldn't be drinking it. Yes, I'm sure it helps you relax and makes you a better dancer, but not all of the effects are positive. I changed my life with a 30-day booze free experiment. Go one week, seven days, without booze and see how it makes you feel. I didn't know how bad I felt until I started feeling better.

For more info on how to make your life better by changing your lifestyle and properly fueling your body visit TerryLancaster.com/fuel.

Get Up Off Of That Thing And Dance 'Til You Feel Better.

5. Train The Machine

———

*Quit Trying To Get Into Better Shape
And Just Be the Shape You're In Better.*

———

We worship daily at the altar of fitness and beauty. Multi-billion dollar industries flood our airwaves and Facebook feeds with images of the beautiful people exercising.

They'll sell us everything we need from thigh masters to gym memberships, from $200 running shoes to the latest and greatest digital doodad that will track every calorie we consume, every step we take, every move me make.

And yet with all that at our disposal two out of three Americans are still overweight or obese, in part because we don't get enough exercise.

It's good business for them. As long as they can keep us focused on the unrealistic ideals and six-pack abs, we'll stay in a constant state of dissatisfaction and keep looking for the magic bullet/weight loss/fitness program to turn it all around.

Oh, look there's a new video that shows us how to get in shape with a scientifically proven 10-minute workout ... and it's only $199. I'm gonna really get serious when it arrives in four to six weeks. In the meantime, pass the Doritos.

We're obsessed with the idea of getting back in shape, the fantasy of working out, but the actual getting up off of the couch and moving around, well, not so much.

But let's flip the script, let's come at it from a different angle.

Let's decide that we're absolutely perfect just the way we are with our love handles and our muffin tops, with our man boobs and our stretch marks, with our thunder thighs and our cottage cheese butt cheeks. And let's decide to work out anyway.

We're an absolute freaking miracle of nature, a wonder to behold, warts and all. And if we can start getting off the couch every once in awhile to work up a sweat, we can be even better.

We don't need to exercise to be pretty, to be thin, to be perfect, get six-pack abs, or be one of the beautiful people.

Let's quit trying to get into shape and just be the shape we're in better.

Exercise makes you smarter.

All the ads tell us we need to exercise to make our bellies smaller and our muscles bigger, but here's a little known fact.

Exercise makes your brain bigger.

"Nothing we know of--no drugs, no activity--nothing else competes with what physical exercise does to increase the number of new brain cells that we make every day," says Harvard professor of psychiatry, Dr. John Ratey, author of *Spark: The Revolutionary New Science of Exercise and the Brain*.

Forget Luminosity. Forget Sudoku. Forget *The New York Times* crossword puzzle. If you really want to increase your mental clarity and sharpness, do a freakin' pushup or two.

As little as four or five minutes of increased cardiovascular activity can stimulate increased blood flow to the brain and spur the growth of new brain cells.

Exercise doesn't just help grow new brain cells, it makes the ones you do have work better

"Exercise improves concentration, attention, motivation, and general overall mood, and decreases impulsivity," says Ratey. "One of the ways that's done is by raising the neurotransmitters dopamine, serotonin, and norepinephrine. A bout of exercise is like taking a little bit of Ritalin and a little bit of Prozac."

A brief bout of exercise can improve your clarity and focus for two to three hours in the short term and help fight brain aging and Alzheimer's in the long run.

So whether you're prepping for a big exam or having a senior moment and can't find any of your seven pairs of reading glasses go for a run. It'll help

Exercise makes you happier.

Everyone's familiar with the concept of the runner's high that occurs when opiate-like endorphins flood the brain with happy juice during exercise, but that's not the whole story.

A quick 20-minute dose of exercise can also help DECREASE production of cortisol, the stress hormone which triggers our instinctive fight or flight response system.

We're rarely battling predators in the wild these days, but the stresses of modern life, from the constant barrage of smartphone notifications to cab drivers cutting us off in traffic, leave our cortisol production in overdrive. With little fleeing and fighting to let our brain know the threat is over, we remain constantly on edge.

Exercise reduces cortisol production by tricking our brain into thinking we've responded to the threat, either by running away or running into battle. Since we've responded, our brain can bring the threat level down from DEFCON 4 and shut off the cortisol spigots.

Less stress means more happy.

That 20-minute jog around the block can leave you in a better mood for up to 12 hours. That's better living through chemistry

And over the long term, a regular exercise regimen is as effective at treating depression as antidepressants like Zoloft according to researchers at Duke University.

Exercise also stimulates the production of brain-derived neurotrophic factor (BDNF) which Dr. Ratey calls "Miracle-Gro for the brain." BDNF repairs the damage caused by constant stress by stimulating new cell growth and strengthening connections in existing cells.

Increased BDNF production is one of the primary method by which SSRI antidepressants (Zoloft, Paxil, Prozac) help patients feel better. Antidepressants are the pharmaceutical industry's Number One Cash Cow. 13% of all Americans are taking prescription antidepressants. Among women ages 50 to 64 that rises to 25%. One out of every four!

We're spending billions on these pills, and they don't accomplish anything that a few dozen jumping jacks can't do!

And it's not just antidepressants. America is the most medicated civilization in the history of, well, civilization.

Nearly 70% of Americans take at least one prescription drug regularly. 50% take two. A mind blowing one out of every five Americans is on five or more prescriptions.

We take them for wide variety of reasons: high blood pressure (22%), high cholesterol (11%), pain (13%), and yes, depression (13%).

Americans like simple solutions: Take this pill and everything will be OK.

Except, here's the thing. The prescriptions don't make everything OK. They don't work.

They aren't even designed to cure anything. They're designed to manage and control chronic conditions. They're designed to lure us into using them everyday for the rest of our lives and lining the pockets of healthcare executives.

And that they do. America spends a higher percentage of our income on healthcare than any other country, ever. And we aren't getting our money's worth. We're one of the least healthy of all developed nations.

Over the last couple of years, I've watched my stepfather die from mismanaged high blood pressure, diabetes, and heart disease because he was counting on the prescriptions to save him, and I've put more than a handful of other family members in the ground from prescription drug overdose.

The prescriptions are not just failing us, they're flat out killing us.

And the saddest part of all is that they're just not necessary. The chronic conditions that Americans are bankrupting themselves to manage with prescription drugs can, in many cases, be treated just as effectively with a two step protocol.

1) Get Up
2) Move Around

The truth is 20 minutes a day of moderate exercise would bankrupt the American healthcare system.

Exercise makes you healthier.

We'd rather take a pill than turn off the TV and get up and take a walk. But getting up off the couch and getting as little as 30 minutes a day of exercise is the single best medical treatment for a whole host of chronic diseases and, just as importantly, the best prevention. Depression, diabetes, high blood pressure, high cholesterol, arthritis and counterintuitively, fatigue.

I've never been a beacon of healthiness. I've been massively overweight for most of my life, but I'm active and healthy. I'm the healthiest morbidly obese dude you'll ever meet. I've grown accustomed to going in for my annual check up and having the nurse check and recheck my blood pressure, tap on the meter, give my rotundness a quick look over and ask "Did you know your blood pressure is perfect?"

Another missed sale because occasionally I get up and do something.

Exercise reduces anxiety, depression and fatigue. Reduces pain. Reduces your chances of debilitating injury. Cuts your risks of developing diabetes, dementia, Alzheimer's Disease, many cancers, and heart disease

That's universal health care!

If the government and the big insurance companies were serious about improving healthcare in this country, someone would be trying to find a way to get America moving ... literally.

Exercise can help you turn your whole sorry life around.

Exercise is what Charles Duhigg, the author of *The Power of Habit* calls a Keystone Habit.

"When people start habitually exercising, even as infrequently as once a week, they start changing other, unrelated patterns in their lives, often unknowingly. Typically people who exercise start eating better and becoming more productive at work. They smoke less and show more patience with colleagues and family. They use their credit cards less frequently and say they feel less stressed."

Little wonder with all the changes in brain chemistry that exercise creates. If you're on a natural high all the time, you'll have a lot less need for smokes, booze and retail therapy.

Exercising more also means cupcakes are less appealing because the sugar junkie in your head already got his fix.

And it's true that exercise gives you more energy--energy to be more productive, tackle new projects, and get more shit done. Exercise is a force multiplier.

Then there's the science of little wins. Accomplishing physical goals as small as running around the block or doing a real live, legit pushup for the first time without resorting to the "knee thing," can give you the confidence you need to step up to new challenges and make other changes in your life.

A while back, I ran a full 5K for the first time in my life.

And I use the term "run" loosely. It was more like a jog or a trot, kind of a shuffle. But what it most definitely was not was a walk. I didn't stop to walk, catch my breath or bend over and vomit. I ran the entire 3.1 miles nonstop.

Now any self-respecting Kenyan could have finished a half marathon in the length of time it took me, but then again, they aren't dragging an eighth of a ton around with them like I am.

Actually, I just checked with my research department (aka Google), and I beat the world record for a half marathon by a full 17 minutes. Woot. Woot.

This is a huge deal for me. Up until then, I had never ran farther than a mile nonstop in my life. Even then, I was the fat kid in last place trying not to let the gym coach catch me stopping.

But I had started out walking around the neighborhood and had gotten fairly diligent about it. I've got a little circuit around the neighborhood that turns out to be exactly 3.1 miles or 5 kilometers, and I was walking that every day.

Somewhere along the way I decided to run a little, just to see if I could.

Starting is the hardest part.

The first day I tried to run any, I barely made it out of my driveway. By the time I got to the end of the street, about 100 yards away, my legs were burning, my heart and my head were pounding and I was huffing and puffing like I had just ran the Boston Marathon and smoked a pack of unfiltered Camels.

So I did what any rational human being who wasn't being chased by a Wooly Mammoth or some other such life threatening creature would do. I stopped running, duh!

The only thing holding me back is me.

Turns out your brain is super, duper logical. And if nobody's chasing you, your brain will offer you every logical reason to stop running.

So I go out the other day to do my 5K, and I'm planning on trying to run a little over half way, that would have still been a new Terry World Record. I'm jogging along for the first half mile or so and I'm not feeling it.

Starting is the hardest part.

A whole litany of excuses, reasons to stop running, was going through my head. I felt OK. Not great. But no one was chasing me so I wanted to stop.

I've got an app on my phone that keeps track of distances and times and keeps a nice little log of all my walks and normally when I get to the far end of the neighborhood, exactly a mile away, a nice, perky female voice gives me a shout out. "1 Mile, Time: blah, blah, blah minutes. Blah, blah, blah seconds"

But when I got to the place where she usually speaks up, this time, I got nothing. So I pulled out my phone and the app had glitched and only recorded 8 tenths of a mile. And the very first thought that went through my little head was "Well, the timer's off, might as well walk now."

Nobody was chasing me so I wanted to stop and I almost did.

But I figured I could get to the mile and half mark and still set a personal record for distance. Of course when I got there, I wanted to stop. The burning was gone from my legs, my heart wasn't pounding. My head didn't hurt and I wasn't huffing and puffing but I still wanted to stop.

The only thing holding me back was me.

I'm not even sure why I kept running. And when my brain wanted me to stop at the two mile mark at the bottom of a half mile long uphill climb, I'm really not sure why I didn't.

But when I made it up that hill and only had a half mile left, I know perfectly good and well why I didn't stop running then.

Winning feels good.

I would hate to think what the neighbors thought if any of them saw me jogging that last half mile.

There was this old fat guy, shuffling down the street, grinning from ear to ear like he had just gotten out of the Magic Mystery Machine with Scooby, Shaggy, Cheech, Chong, Bob Marley, and the entire cast of "Dazed and Confused."

My only consolation is that they couldn't hear the "Rocky" Soundtrack that was going on in my head. It was all I could do to keep from bobbing, weaving and shadow boxing. I'll have to admit that when I took the steps up the front porch, I took them two at a time, with my fists pumping in the air. Bah Bah Bah. The chorus from "Eye of the Tiger" stuck on repeat in my head.

Winning feels good.

The confidence I gained that day has helped me to make other massive changes in my life. I'm off the booze. I'm off the sugar. I've slashed my TV viewing by half or more.

Exercise will change your life. Period. No question about it.

Dropping a few pounds and fitting into your skinny jeans? Well, that's just a happy little side effect.

But if exercise is such a simple way to improve our lives, why don't more of us exercise?

Marathoners and other endurance athletes talk about "hitting the wall," when their body has done all it can do, burned up all its energy and just gives up. For a fine tuned athlete that could happen 15-20 miles into a 26-mile race.

For most people I hang out with, "The Wall" happens somewhere between the couch and the table we left the remote on.

Getting started is the hardest part, and I can't tell you any way to make getting started any easier, but I can tell you one 100%

guaranteed, sure-fire way to make it simpler, and I can tell you three reasons that keep most of us from doing just that.

We're trying to be what we're not.

I'm assuming you're not a world-class athlete trying to shave a hundredth of a second off your personal best time. Quit worrying about them, what they do and how they train. You're not playing in the same league. You're not even playing the same game.

Same for your friends who are running marathons or working out five days a week alternating cardio days, leg days, and upper body days. They have no useful wisdom to share for those of us just struggling to get off the couch.

I'm fat, out of shape, and clinging to middle aged by the thinnest of demographics margins. A few months ago, I couldn't run to the mailbox, much less a marathon.

Accept who you are and concentrate on being you better.

We're trying to do what we can't.

I used to play hockey with a guy in Nashville who started playing at the age of 30 and decided he wanted to make it to the NHL (most of us hockey players aren't terribly bright). He booked an appointment with a professional coach and wanted to discuss a training/coaching regimen that would get him league ready in the quickest time.

The coach told him he should build a time machine and start playing hockey every day at the age of 3. Play your way up through pee wee, bantam, midget, and Juniors. And try to be born in Canada.

Now maybe with hard work, dedication, proper nutrition, professional training, and a little good fortune, this guy was the one in a billion guy who could make it. It's not likely, but maybe. I do know this, if he'd have just set out to play old fart hockey a couple of nights a week, hang out with his friends, and be a better middle-aged beer leaguer he'd probably still be playing hockey and having a blast today. I haven't seen him around the rink in 10 years.

Maybe you can run a marathon if that's what you really want to do. And maybe you can swim the English channel and hike the Appalachian Trail. But if you're hitting the wall somewhere between the couch and the remote, running a marathon isn't what you need to be thinking about.

The no pain, no gain bullshit.

After I ran that first 3.1 miles and started running more regularly, thoughts started popping in my head that maybe I should train harder, really push myself to run a half, maybe even a full marathon. And maybe I should.

But I found out when I ran farther and faster, a lot of the times, I felt worse. I didn't have the energy left to do things I really wanted to do. And I watched a lot of my friends push themselves harder than their eighth of a ton middle-aged bodies could handle, and they ended up injuring themselves and going back to the couch where it always feels safe and warm.

Yesterday was a beautiful day in Nashville--56 degrees and sunny after weeks and weeks of freezing, drizzling, and cloudy. I went outside, ran two miles, and it felt glorious. I felt good all day, I had more energy all day, and I'm not sore today so I'm good to go play hockey with my buddies tonight.

I could run farther and faster. I could push myself harder. I could lose more weight. But that's not why I run.

I run to feel better and I've figured out that if I just concentrate on the that, everything else will take care of itself.

Quit trying to be something you're not.

Quit trying to do something you can't.

Quit trying to get into shape, into better shape, or into some other shape and just start, today, being in the shape you're in, better.

Starting is the hardest part.

The answer isn't easy. But it is as simple as putting down the remote, getting off your ass and doing something, anything really ... today.

And by anything, I mean, you know, anything ... Naked Yoga, for instance.

I used to go out for a typical American lunch most days: cheeseburger, fries, and a Coke. These days, I mostly spend lunch hour at home, on my deck, doing Naked Yoga.

Two things you need to know about Naked Yoga: I'm not actually naked and it's not actually yoga.

But Scantily Clad Stretching and Jumping Around just doesn't quite have the same ring to it.

The guys on my hockey team get quite a kick out of the idea of my naked fat ass outside doing yoga poses. I'm convinced that a couple of them periodically look up my address on Google Maps in hopes that the satellite caught me in an ill-timed Downward Facing Dog pose.

I'm all about propagating The Legend of Terry. But the truth is when I'm outside doing my daily routine, I am wearing clothing, just not much. And definitely not enough to make my neighbors feel comfortable were they to accidentally catch the show.

One of the main benefits, the main reason I do it, is to feel the sun shining on my skin. There are a whole host of benefits to sunlight, not the least of which is that 30 minutes of sunshine on your skin will release about as much serotonin (your brain's happy juice) as that Whopper Combo meal I used to wolf down on the daily.

Sunlight is health and happiness in a bottle, without the bottle.

A little sun on your face and hands won't do the trick. So off comes the shirt and on go the little, tiny Richard Simmons shorts to barely cover my round mound of rebound. Sorry about the visual.

I've actually taken a handful of yoga classes and I've watched some videos, so I know what actual yoga is supposed to be. This isn't it. I don't have an instructor or video player out on the deck with me, and I'm kind of an anti-authoritarian, screw the regimen, freestyle kind of guy any way.

So Naked Yoga is mostly freestyle which makes it hard to describe and probably even harder to witness, so if you do ever come over to my house around lunch time, please call first for your own benefit.

When I first started exercising a little my entire goal was to break a sweat every day. And quite honestly, of all the changes I've made in my life over the last couple of years, breaking a sweat every day is the one that has made all the others possible.

I start things off by breaking a sweat. I jump around, jog in place, imaginary jump rope, a little shadow boxing, a few kicks, a few high knees and my favorite, wide stance, side to side jogging in place. Basically I mimic the ice skating stride so I'm breaking a sweat and building up my skating muscles at the same time. A twofer!

After maybe ten minutes, my heart rate is elevated and I start to sweat a little. It doesn't take long to glisten in the Tennessee sunshine.

Now comes the stretch.

I'm convinced that stretching most days has taken about 15-20 years off the way I feel every day. I used to play hockey and be tired, rundown, and sore for 2-3 days afterward. Now when I get a good stretch in on game days, I play much better hockey and on days after, I stretch the tired and sore right out of my body.

I start by reaching to the sky, both hands fully extended. Taking deep breaths. Arms to the side, rotate my body right and left. Rotate my neck and shoulders. And hit all 4 points on the compass with hip rotations/thrusts. I'm sure this is particularly attractive. Then hands on the ground, ass in the air, knees fully straight. Breathe in. Breathe out. And pull my head as close to my knees as I can get.

I finish up with a couple of knee bends and a lunge in each direction with arms overhead and again with arms to each side rotating.

It's all free style so it changes up from day to day based on what feels like it needs stretching, but the main idea is to get everything as fully extended as possible in every direction with deep, deep breaths in and out to expand my lung capacity.

For balance I stand on my tippy toes with arms stretched to the sky and then to the side and hold that for as many breaths as I can. My calves are monsters now!

Then I do the prototypical yoga pose that you see in every yoga brochure. It's called TREE POSE. And basically you balance on one leg while resting the other foot on your inner thigh. I actually cup my instep on the knee. It fits nicely, and that's about all the flexibility I've got. If you can get your heel up around your junk, good on ya!

I hold that pose for a few breaths with my hands overhead and then move my arms out to the side and turn my head in each direction to change my point of focus. That requires some serious concentration.

Then I extend my leg fully to the front for a few breaths, into a full side kick and finally one leg fully extended to the rear, my back horizontal to the ground and my arms fully extended to the front. The yoga books call it the Warrior pose, but to me it should be called Superman.

I move back into a tall standing position and switch legs to do it all over again.

If 10 minutes of shadowboxing doesn't get you sweating, this will. Balancing on one leg works almost every muscle in your body because you're making thousands of tiny adjustments every second to maintain the balance.

If you've ever scoffed at yoga as something for soccer moms, try this one time. You won't scoff anymore.

The whole thing takes about 30 minutes. On days I do it, I feel like a million bucks. On days I don't get to, I never seem to have as much giddyup and go. And that's the only reason I do it. Because it makes me feel good.

I did this routine for a year and only lost handful of pounds but it changed the way I felt and gave me the energy to add in some walking and eventually running which has helped me drop 60 pounds. In all honesty, though, the weight loss is distant, distant second to how I feel.

And in the immortal words of the late, great James Brown, "I Feel Good!"

If you're not currently leading an active lifestyle, then getting up out of the chair, off the couch, away from the screen, and moving around is probably the easiest most effective change you can make to improve your life.

There's an economics joke (Now there's an oxymoron!) that describes lotteries as a tax on stupid people. But the economists need to double check their math. I'm no mathematician, but I know that any chance, no matter how small, no matter how astronomically stacked the odds are against me ... Any chance is better than no chance at all.

Some is better than none.

You gotta play to win.

BETTER!

Dropping a buck on a chance to win a few million bucks is a no brainer. And dropping that first buck improves my chances INFINITELY over not having any shot at all. Dropping that first buck, taking the first step, is a game changer.

The same thing goes for exercise.

Taking that first step away from the couch and out into the world of movement, that's where you get the biggest bang for your buck.

I've got a newsflash for you. Your couch is perfectly capable of holding itself down on the ground. It doesn't need your ass parked on it 24 hours a day to keep from floating off into space. You're not doing it any favors just sitting there, and you aren't doing yourself any favors either.

You can start building a dramatically better life today just by limiting the amount of time you spent with your ass in a seat and your face in a screen.

I'm not talking about building a home fitness center, joining classes, or running a marathon.

I'm talking about just getting up off your hiney and doing something, anything! For 30 minutes a day.

Take a walk around the block, dance around your office, do the dishes by hand, park on the other side of the parking lot.

Being active for 30 minutes a day gives you amazing health benefits that are nothing short of miraculous and yet they pale in comparison to the changes it can make in the way you feel.

I know you're tired when you get home from work and you're too busy during the day to actually get up off your ass, but I guaran-damn-tee you, that if you'll push yourself to get up and move, you'll not deplete your precious energy. You'll create more!

If you'll take the time out of your day for just a tiny little bit of exercise, you'll make more time by getting more done, being able to focus better and being more productive. You're not wasting your precious time, you're investing in your own efficiency.

You are designed for motion. And being in motions helps keep the machine in tune.

But most importantly being in motion just 30 minutes a day will make you happier.

Being even just slightly more in shape than you are now will put some spring in your step. You'll just plain feel better. You'll look better. You'll BE better.

And that will make you happier.

Some is better than none and a journey of a thousand miles begins with a single step.

Get to steppin'.

ACTION STEPS

1) TAKE A HIKE. Get outside today and go for a walk. It doesn't matter how far. It doesn't matter how fast. What matter is that you got up off the couch and did it.

2) TAKE ANOTHER HIKE. Get outside TOMORROW and go for a walk. It doesn't matter how far. It doesn't matter how fast. But it does matter how often. Repeat daily.

3) PLANK. Get down on the floor, on your toes and elbows, and hold yourself in plank position for as long as you can. I hold a plank every morning while my coffee is brewing.

4) THIS IS THE PART ON SPROCKETS WHEN WE DANCE. Take a dance break at the office. Get up. Crank It Up. And shake your moneymaker.

5) STAND UP AND STRETCH. Stand up as tall as you can for just a minute. Imagine that your head is attached to a helium balloon, pulling it straighter and straighter. Higher and higher. Now raise your arms up as high as you can. With every breath, try to reach a little higher. Up on your Tippy toes. Reach and don't forget to breathe.

6) TOESIE WOESIES. When's the last time you took a good look at your toes? Let's take a look now, shall we? Feet shoulder width apart. Knees straight, bend over and reach to the ground. Now take a deep breath and as you exhale let your arms sink closer to your toes. If you can't reach them, just wave. Breather again and sink a little deeper. Reach.

6) DROP AND GIVE ME ONE. Have you peed today? That's what I thought. Somebody owes me a pushup!

For more info on how to exercise is the keystone habit to build your better life around visit TerryLancaster.com/exercise.

Quit Letting An Imaginary There And Then
Screw Up A Perfectly Good Here And Now.

6. Get Your Head Out Of Your Head

—

Tell Your Brain That It's Not The Boss Of You.

—

A guy goes to the doctor's office to complain about his shoulder.

"Doc, it hurts every time I do this."

"Well," says the doctor. "Don't do that anymore. That'll be $275."

Ba Da Bing!!

That's funny right?

We all like to think we've got enough sense to avoid intentionally doing things that are physically painful. But things that are emotionally or psychologically painful, that's a whole 'nother something.

There's a Bob Newhart skit floating around on YouTube where he reprises his role as a psychiatrist. A female patient walks into his office and tells him that her life is in shambles because of her fear of being buried alive in a box. She thinks about it constantly to the detriment of everything else in her life.

Newhart tells her that he has two words that can solve all her problems as long as she remembers them and applies them to her life after she leaves the office.

STOP IT!

"But, when I was a kid ..."

STOP IT!

"But my mother used to ..."

STOP IT!

"But every night I dream ..."

STOP IT!

That'll be $275

Mark Tewart is a sales trainer, author, and professional speaker who uses STOP IT! as a mantra for salespeople and sales managers to cut out the excuses, to cut out the negative self-talk, to quit rationalizing failure and get busy getting busy!

It sounds simple and it is.

But it ain't easy.

Your brain is like a dog with a bone, and when negative thoughts creep in, they tend to stay there.

We all have an ongoing narration track running in our heads. An inner voice. The little man behind the curtain. Only our Narrator rarely seems to talk about what's going on right now.

More often than not, our inner Narrator goes off on a tangent, reliving the past or imagining the future.

My own personal Narrator loves to think of snappy comebacks to arguments I might have had weeks before. It goes round and round crafting the perfect talking points over and over and over again.

Some Narrators are perpetual worry-warts, playing an endless stream of what-if scenarios. What if I get sick? What if I lose my job?

And some Narrators are the Johnny Paychecks of internal monologues. They spend hours upon hours rephrasing the perfect way to tell our bosses to "Take This Job And Shove It," and telling everyone else who has perturbed us in one way or another just exactly where the line of people who can kiss our ass starts.

A study from the Harvard School of Medicine finds that on average our mind wanders 47% of the time. We spend half of our waking life disengaged from reality and living in an imaginary world.

We get so distracted listening to the voices in our heads that we are rarely fully present in our actual lives. How many times have you completely missed your exit on the interstate because you were "lost in thought"?

We keep letting a totally imaginary there and then screw up a perfectly good here and now.

The Narrator is rarely a happy camper. Most of the thoughts that get stuck on repeat in our heads are the negative kind, much like a scab that has to be picked at or a "wobbly tooth" that must be wiggled every few seconds to make sure it's still irritating. And it always is.

And when The Narrator is happy, it's rarely about the way things are. He wanders off into the future on flights of fantasy about how our lives could be just perfect ... if only this, that, or the other thing would happen.

And like a top 40 station that only plays 27 songs, you get to hear the same thing all day, every day, whether that's what you really want to hear or not.

But what if I were to tell you there was a request line? What if you really could tell the little man in your head to just STOP IT!

Well you can. It's simple. But it ain't easy.

That's why you have to work at it.

We readily accept the idea that we have to train our body to get it to do what we want. To strengthen our muscles, we have to use our muscles. But few of us apply the same logic to our brain.

Your brain is the most powerful organism in the known universe. The human brain can create marvels and destroy civilizations.

It can make your life a paradise or a prison.

Shouldn't you spend as much time training it as you do working on your biceps?

That's all meditation is. Training for your brain.

Or maybe more accurately it's brain taming: teaching the yappy little Chihuahua in your head to shut the hell up every once in awhile.

The purpose of meditation is to become intimately familiar with the present moment. Fully aware and mindful of the way things are right now.

But the major benefit of meditation is understanding that the voice in your head, the one that's been leading you around since you were 3 or 4 years old isn't you. It's just the announcer. The disc jockey. The storyteller. The Narrator.

Meditation can help reset the default mode of the brain from endlessly pursuing every random thought the Narrator whispers in your inner ear to a state of being more fully aware of what's happening right now, more fully present in this moment of your life or, as the gurus would call it, more in the now.

"I can't do that," my friends tell me when I explain meditation as a method for learning to gently push aside all the thoughts that creep into our heads.

STOP IT!

Of course you can't do that. You've never even tried. You've never practiced. You haven't put in the work.

You pushed play on the little voice in your head as soon as you learned to talk, and he hasn't shut up since. He's had free reign for decades, and you expect him to shut up the first time you ask?

But with a little training and with a little practice, you can learn to observe, acknowledge, and ignore The Narrator. You can make him shut up when he needs to shut up. You can make him talk about things that will help you in the real world. And when he starts talking about all the negative crap he's so fond of, you can make him STOP IT!

You can get your head out of your head, one thought at a time.

When Andy Puddicombe was a boy he went with his mother to a meditation class, which in his 11-year-old mind meant he would be learning some Kung Fu, Jedi, Super Ninja type stuff, possibly even how to levitate and fly.

He did not learn how to fly.

But the concept of mindfulness and learning to control your own thought patterns stuck with him as he later travelled the world, became a Buddhist monk, and went on to found Headspace, a $50 million startup devoted to bringing mindfulness to the masses and the celebrity set, including Emma Watson and Gwyneth Paltrow, both advocates of his 10-minute mindfulness app.

So if meditating can't teach you to levitate or fly, if meditation simply teaches you to observe, acknowledge, and ignore the never ending stream of chatter in your mind, why bother?

Because the benefits of learning how to tune in and tune out at will are anything but simple.

By learning to ignore the random thoughts that pop into our head, we can focus our energy, focus our efforts, and get more done in less time without stopping to Google the name of that movie David Spade was in. You know, the one where he had the mullet and the Camaro. And just how tall is David Spade anyway? I wonder if he's taller than Tom Cruise. Prince?

Our modern world is a constant stream of distractions and with the sum total of all human knowledge just a mouse click away, there is literally no more valuable talent than the ability to stay on task. Meditation can help you do that.

We live in a frantic, stressful world filled with a barrage of stimuli, from cell phones buzzing to the 24-hour news cycle. Our bodies weren't designed for the stress of modern living, and it keeps our fight or flight response in a constant state of emergency preparedness: our hearts pump faster; our blood pressure increases, muscles tighten and tense. Meanwhile our everyday non-emergency functions like digestion and immunity suffer while we wait for the next explosion of stimuli.

Stress, and the resulting higher cortisol levels and inflammation, are factors in many chronic conditions: heart disease, high blood pressure, obesity, even cancer.

For years, inflammation has been treated as symptom of these diseases, but we're starting to realize that it may be the actual cause. Inflammation occurs when your body perceives a threat and your internal defenses gather together to mass a defense against allergens and infections.

And if the constant attack from the outside world weren't stressful enough, our brains are addicted to constant stimulation and narrative. If they're not getting it from the world, they'll just make it up with the little man in your head screaming his best Chicken Little impersonation 16 waking hours a day: The Sky is Falling! The Sky is Falling!

We recount every altercation, every missed opportunity and disappointment, remembered, anticipated, or imagined, over and over and over again, keeping our stress levels high right along with our blood pressure and heart rate.

We let our resentments for the past and our worry for the future cannibalize our enjoyment of the present.

But we can STOP IT!

Meditation can lower our dependence on prescription drugs to ward off depression and anxiety, and it can also lower blood pressure and pain response.

Perhaps even more importantly, meditation can improve our own internal immune function, at a cellular level, by switching on disease fighting genes, and at a system wide level by lowering our DEFCON 4 Fight or Flight emergency response status and letting our immune system get the resources it needs to do the its job.

People who meditate, even in small amounts, have measurably lower levels of the stress hormone cortisol. And lower levels of inflammation

The research has proven, over and over, that meditation and mindfulness can boost your immune system, lower your blood pressure, and rewire parts of your brain, growing extra gray matter in the areas associated with self awareness and compassion and shrinking the parts of your brain associated with stress.

Finally meditating can make you happier. In fact, meditation fundamentally rewires your brain to remain in a natural state of happiness.

It only makes sense. Happiness is an internal function depending almost entirely on how we react to the outside reality of our lives. Learning to observe, acknowledge and ignore our reactions to the outside world gives us the power to make happiness a choice.

We can choose to cuss, spit, and shake our fist at the asshole who cut us off THREE exits ago on the interstate.

Or we can observe that cursing and spitting is not increasing our happiness and we can choose to just let it go.

We have that power. We've had it all along.

Meditation is just practice for controlling our emotions when they need to be controlled.

You may not learn how to fly.

You may not learn how to levitate.

But meditating for just five to 10 minutes a day can help you be healthier, happier, and more productive all day long.

And that, my friend, is some real life, genuine Kung Fu, Jedi, Super

Ninja type stuff.

In 2004, Dan Harris was a fidgety, type A, hard-charging war correspondent for ABC News, freshly back from the front lines and adjusting to life behind a desk but still in front of the cameras.

One Saturday morning, he was the anchoring the news segment on Good Morning America, a job he loved, a job he had been born to do, when the unthinkable happened. He panicked. In front of 5.019 million viewers. More precisely he suffered a panic attack. His heart began to race. His chest tightened. His breathing became shallow and labored. And he started to sweat.

Richard-Nixon-getting-his-ass-handed-to-him-by-JFK sweat.

Albert-Brooks-in-Broadcast-News sweat.

Justin-Bieber-first-night-in-prison sweat.

The whole incident only lasted seconds before he royally confused the producers by sending the cameras back to the GMA hosts, whom he proceeded to call by the wrong name.

It might have only been seconds for the millions of viewers. But inside your head, those seconds can seem like a near eternity.

While excessive sweating and panting may be a plus for some on screen performers (cough, porn), it's a definite liability in the calm, cool, and collected world of talking heads and network news. So Dan sought psychiatric advice to help make sure it didn't happen again.

His panic attack, it turns out, was a result of excessive adrenaline in his brain, a by-product of his type-A personality, the stresses of big time journalism, and a little casual cocaine and ecstasy use.

"My on-air meltdown was the direct result of an extended run of mindlessness," says Harris, "a period of time during which I was focused on advancement and adventure, to the detriment of pretty much everything else in my life."

Around the same time, Peter Jennings approached Harris to increase ABC News' coverage of religion, a difficult role for the secular son of scientists, an avowed agnostic who only took part in his Bar Mitzvah for the money.

His new assignment at work gave him cover to pursue a better understanding of what had caused his panic attack. Eventually he met and interviewed new age gurus like Deepak Chopra and Eckhart Tolle who introduced him to the concept of the inner Narrator that keeps us distracted from fully living in the present moment. The inner voice that had led Harris to push himself harder and faster to prove himself at work. The same voice that convinced him that a little coke would give him the extra edge he needed. The same voice that ultimately led to his panic attack in front of millions of viewers.

Meditation and mindfulness, they told him, could help quiet the voice in his head. The problem was the packaging. The gurus mixed pseudo science and psycho babble willy-nilly. You could almost hear the babbling brooks and pan flute music when they spoke.

"I thought of meditation as the exclusive province of bearded swamis, unwashed hippies, and fans of John Tesh music," Dan Harris writes in his book 10% Happier, a book he originally wanted to call, *The Voice In My Head Is An Asshole*.

But the more he researched, the more he found that the flowing robes and incense smoke of the gurus were hiding a treasure trove of genuine scientific research showing the benefits of meditation and mindfulness.

And it was the research that swayed this son of scientists.

Harris went from scoffing at meditation to dipping his toes. Then from being a daily practitioner to becoming an evangelist.

10% Happier is one of Amazon's top-selling books on meditation, although it still trails Tolle's *The Power of Now*.

He predicts that meditation may be the next big thing in personal health, and that just a few years from now could be as widely accepted as daily exercise and multi-vitamins, IF we can work on the image problem.

He wants to bring meditation to the masses.

And ditch the pan flutes.

I don't live on a mountain top

I don't own a silk robe.

I haven't burned any incense since the 70s.

I'm a redneck hockey player born and raised in the Deep South.

And I meditate every day.

Not for long, maybe 15 minutes or so out on my deck in the sunshine.

On a good day all I hear is birds chirping and the distant drone of highway traffic.

On a bad day one next door neighbor is having a roof installed by a dozen workers with two hammers each and no sense of rhythm. While the other neighbor has a landscaping crew over with two nuclear-powered, turbocharged, zero radius mowers and three leaf blowers with new and improved cyclone force power.

Either way, the process is the same and as simple as 1, 2, 3.

1) Focus solely on breathing in and out.

Sit or stand and become aware of your breathing. Breathe deeply at whatever pace and rhythm feels natural. Concentrate on the breath entering your nose, filling your lungs, expanding your chest and diaphragm, and then reversing course as your chest deflates and the breath exits your body. Concentrate on your extremities, your arms, your legs, your hands, your feet, your toes, your fingers, and imagine the oxygen traveling all throughout your body.

Breathe in. Breathe out.

2) Gradually you'll become aware of other thoughts and observations creeping into your consciousness.

The dog's barking next door. There's a plane flying overhead. The electric bill is due tomorrow. That guy who cut you off in traffic this morning was a giant freaking asshole and he's lucky you didn't go all FALLING DOWN road rage on him.

And then there's work. And your spouse. And little Johnny's failing algebra. And a thousand other thoughts every second, every day in a constant, never-ending stream.

And it's easy to obsess on them. It's easy to get frustrated once you become more and more aware that they are always there and you're supposed to be concentrating on breathing in and out and your damn brain just won't shut up.

The voice in your head is like rain on an old roof. Constantly searching for a way in. Exploring every nook and cranny. The thoughts come back. They always do.

But there's no reason to obsess or get frustrated. God gave us these big brains so we can have big thoughts. It's completely natural for your brain to be broadcasting all the time. That's what it does.

Your brain exists to create narrative out of nothing. It finds the storyline in the chaos.

The point of meditation is learning to choose which broadcasts we listen to.

So when you become aware of the myriad thoughts creeping into your head, acknowledge them, choose to ignore them, and

3) Repeat step one.

ACTION STEPS

1) TAKE A BIG DEEP BREATH. Right here. Right Now. Breathe in through your nose. Slowly. Deeply. Feel your chest expand as it fills with air Breathe out through your mouth. Slowly. Slowly. Push the air out hard so it makes that little whooshing noise. Feel your chest deflate and your shoulders sag as the air leaves your body.

2) TUNE INTO YOUR HEAD. Listen in like you're eavesdropping on the couple in the next booth at Red Lobster. Just listen. Don't judge. Let the thoughts bounce around however they want. Observe how one thought leads to another. How random bits pop in here and there. How the same snippets, vague hints of ideas, and thoughts appear over and over again sometimes as just barely formed suggestions of a memory of a thought you once had. Just this once, give the narrator free range and watch him dance.

3) TAKE 10 DEEP BREATHS. The same as before. In through your nose. Out through your mouth counting ONE as you listen to the whoosh of breath leaving your body. And again. And again.

4) TUNE INTO YOUR HEAD AGAIN. But this time understand that you're pulling the strings. You are the puppet master. Listen and observe the thoughts going past and when a negative thought creeps in ... STOP IT! Tell your head that you don't want to think that thought and observe how you stop thinking it. recognize that power. It's an awesome feeling.

5) QUIT YOUR BITCHING. Your thoughts become your words and your words become your thoughts. It's a vicious feedback cycle, so tomorrow do everything in your power not to say anything negative. No complaining. No bitching. No moaning. When you recognize the negative thoughts on the tip of your tongue, put them aside. Take a deep breath. And think happy thoughts!

6) TAKE 50 DEEP BREATHS. The same as before. In and out. In and out. Every time a new thought pops in your head observe it, acknowledge it and then put it aside focusing back on the next deep breath. In and out. And don't get lost in the counting. Your focus shouldn't be on the numbers. Focus on the breath. Each one after the other.

For more info on training your brain and telling the little man in your head to just STOP IT! Visit TerryLancaster.com/meditation.

Live Every Moment Of Your Life
Like It's Your Full Time Job.

7. Be Here Now

And Become The Master Of Your Domain.

Someone asked me once why I liked hockey so much. This was way back, before I had the slightest idea what Zen was or had any idea at all about meditation or being one with the universe. What I told him was this:

When I'm playing hockey, there's no room for anything else in my head. I don't have time to think about anything but chasing the puck and trying to avoid bodily harm.

The guy who asked me the question was mainly confused that I didn't share his passion for golf. I explained that golf, to me, was three hours of my mind wandering, focusing on anything and everything except the task at hand, interrupted a few times to swing a stick.

But hockey is almost all non-stop action from the moment your skates hit the ice until the moment your ass hits the bench. Your mind doesn't have time think about anything but playing hockey. Pucks are whizzing around, grown ass men are careening by at the outer limits of their speed, agility, and control. There's no time to think about the ass chewing your boss gave you earlier that day or the argument you had with your wife or whether or not you remembered to pay the credit card bill in time to avoid the late fees. For the 90 seconds or so that you're on the ice, hockey is all there is.

And for the 90 seconds after that you're trying to catch your breath.

Then your buddy comes flying over the boards, your skates land back on the ice, and you're lost again in the world of stick and puck.

Happiness is the degree to which your external reality, what's happening in front of your eyeballs, matches your internal reality, what's happening between your earholes.

If that's what happiness is, then I can honestly say I'm never happier than when I'm playing hockey.

Ancient Chinese monks and that Grasshopper dude from Kung Fu might call it ZEN, but modern day psychologists call it FLOW, the mental state when you are fully immersed in an activity--engaged, focused, and energized. Lost in the moment.

Have you ever been driving down the interstate, basically driving on autopilot, so lost completely in whatever inner narrative is going on between your earholes that you just drive right past your exit?

FLOW is the exact opposite of that: When you are so consumed by the task at hand that there's no room in your head to think of anything else. Except that thinking isn't exactly the right word.

When you're in a FLOW state, you're not THINKING of anything, you're just doing. Being.

Malcolm Gladwell's book *Blink* is about our ability to think without thinking, how sometimes we just know the right answer. We know what to do. Especially when we've reached FLOW.

I tell all the guys on my hockey team, "There's no thinking in hockey."

If you ever notice a thought crossing your brain in the middle of a hockey game:

"Davey's breaking, I should pass to him";

"The goalie is a leftie, I need to deke left and go backhand to his glove side";

if you have time to think that thought, you've missed the opportunity to do that thing.

And if two equally good options present themselves at the exact same moment--pass to Davey or go glove side on the goalie-- sometimes your brain will stutter step, attempt to think on its own, completely average the two options and you'll end up splitting the difference and shooting the puck almost exactly halfway between Davey and that damn left-handed goalie.

I've seen it happen a thousand times. Not thinking is harder than it sounds.

A lot of what I used to chalk up to being lucky on the ice is actually a result of this thinking without thinking--FLOW.

The ancient Chinese monks from Kung Fu have another phrase for this too: *wu wei*, which translates roughly as action without action.

The thing is you can't learn to reach *flow*, you can't try to be *zen*, you can't think yourself to *wu wei*.

There's a story about the Yoga instructor whose student complained that no matter how long he practiced Yoga, no matter how hard he tried, he couldn't reach enlightenment and maybe the instructor should teach him something new to help.

The instructor responded: "Quit trying so hard and just do the damn stretches."

I'm pretty sure that's what Yoda meant when he said, "There is no try. Either do or do not."

Trying is concentrating on the outcome. The expected result. And expectations are the enemy of happiness.

Doing focuses your mind, your body, your entire reality on the activity, on the task at hand.

If you want to lose yourself in the moment …

If you want to get more done ...

If you want to reach FLOW ...

Quit trying so hard and do the damn thing, whatever the damn thing is.

Just Do It.

And the only way to do it is to do it.

But first, you have to *start* doing it.

Tom Petty was wrong: the waiting is not the hardest part.

The hardest part is starting. Almost always.

Whether it's getting up out of bed to go for a run, writing a blog post, or picking up the phone to cold call new sales prospects, overcoming inertia and actually taking that first action is the tough part.

That's the bad news; the good news is, once you actually get started, inertia goes to work for you.

An object at rest tends to remain at rest, and an object in motion tends to remain in motion.

Starting is the hardest part.

I've found a magic trick that helps me get my ass in gear, overcome inertia, and get started on many of the little tweaks I'm making in Terry World. It's called the Pomodoro Technique.

The Pomodoro Technique was originally thought up in the late 80's as a time management technique. It's named after the little red tomato kitchen timers. You break your work into 25-minute chunks (pomodori) and work on the task at hand without interruption. Then you take a three-to-four-minute break and jump back in for another 25-minute round. Twenty-five minutes is said to be the optimum time for human attention, and the commitment to work without interruption on a single task improves your focus and let's you slip into flow … the state where everything comes naturally and you are completely absorbed in the present moment.

And yes, without interruption means no phone calls, no checking the email, no twitters, No LOL's at your sister's best friend's cute kitten meme on Facebook. Twenty-five minutes doing one thing.

I've come to think of it as the Charles Emerson Winchester III rule. For everyone younger than me, and that mostly means everyone, Charles Emerson Winchester III was a character on the long running TV show M*A*S*H. He was a snooty, upper crust Boston surgeon who eschewed the frolicky banter and multi-tasking the other surgeons in their Korean War medical unit participated in.

Instead, he calmly and methodically would "do one thing at a time. Do it very well. Then move on."

The Pomodoro Technique is just the simple strategy of focusing all of your attention on one activity for a limited amount of time ... and then moving on.

If you want to sell more stuff, spend one hour cold calling new customers and then move on.

If you need to get more organized, set aside 25 minutes, turn off the phone, turn off the TV, shut down the computer, and spend 25 minutes doing nothing but getting organized.

Everyone likes to think that we're all master multitaskers, that we can do it all at the same time and nothing will suffer for it. We're not. Multitasking is an urban myth. Give it up and focus.

The Pomodoro technique is an invaluable tool for time management, productivity, improving focus, and fighting the siren song of multi-tasking. But I've found it to be most useful for overcoming that initial hurdle. To get me started. Twenty-five minutes isn't that long; I can talk my brain into starting if I promise to only work for 25 minutes.

I don't actually have a little red tomato timer, but there are hundreds of apps and websites with built in timers to help you use the technique. I'm sure there's a timer app on your phone right now. If not, simply type SET TIMER FOR 25 MINUTES into Google; it has a timer built in that gets the job done.

I've used the 25-minute rule to help me get started doing dozens of things that I used to put off. Like writing for instance. The timer just dinged and I'm 477 words in for this session. This is where I differ in practice from the original theory. I should be stopping to take a little three-to-four-minute break, but I'm in flow, the words are flying out of my fingers, and I don't want to stop to lose that mojo. So I'm going to cheat a little and keep at it for a few more minutes.

I've also used Pomodori to motivate me to exercise, clean my office, organize my desk, cold call on customers, work on bookkeeping, meditate. All of the stuff I used to put off, now I'll just set a timer and jump right in.

When I'm writing, like now, I'll tend to go over time and want to keep going … but on stuff I really, really hate, like bookkeeping and organizing, I've found that if I set my timer, roll up my sleeves and get to work, all that stuff I've been putting off for weeks can actually get done in less than 25 minutes. I'll find myself 17 minutes into a Pomodori actually looking for something else to clean wondering why I'd been putting this off for three-and-a-half weeks.

It's amazing how many of life's little problems can be solved with 25 minutes of concentrated effort.

We procrastinate. And the procrastination causes dread. And the dread causes worry. And worry causes stress. And stress can kill you.

So set a timer. Get started. And get more shit done.

In Chapter 6, we learned that most of us spend around half our lives lost in thought, wandering around the nooks and crannies in our mind, mostly oblivious to the real world right in front of our nose. And we learned mindfulness techniques and meditation practices to help us train our brain to stay focused on the things we want to focus on.

That skill and the Pomodoro technique will go a long way toward keeping you in a state of flow much more often.

Not all the time, though.

The brain's urge to wander is powerful, especially when the task at hand is boring and doesn't require all of our brain power. I hope your job engages you fully and keeps you alert, focused, and in flow eight hours a day. For most everyone, that's not the case.

But what if our lives depended on paying attention even when we're bored?

For military and for law enforcement personnel it often does. The even have a saying for it:

Stay Alert and Stay Alive.

I've often heard police work and military service described as months of mind-numbing boredom sprinkled with random moments of sheer terror.

The tedium prevents them from reaching flow and getting lost in the actual moment that's actually happening, and I'm sure empires have fallen because one mind wandered at the wrong time.

Modern soldiers are now trained to periodically reacquaint themselves with the present moment by taking an SLLS break.

Stop. Look. Listen. Smell.

Infantry platoons will stop, take a knee, and engage their senses moving nothing but head in a circular arc scanning the surrounding area.

My youngest daughter is a lifeguard and lives depend on her teenage brain not wandering. So lifeguards are trained to do essentially the same thing as the soldiers. She has to scan the entire pool every ten seconds in a pattern like she was mowing the lawn. All the way across and all the way back. And she has to move her head, not just her eyes, to keep herself fully engaged.

She hasn't mentioned anything about smelling.

But soldiers claim that with regular practice all of your senses become heightened even smell. One soldier told the story of being alone in the woods on maneuvers miles from civilization when he stopped for an SLLS break and was almost overpowered by the smell of peanut butter. Peanut Butter.

By following the smell for a hundred yards he was able to sneak up on an unsuspecting sentry quietly enjoying a midnight snack, while I'm sure his mind wandered.

I've never been a soldier or a cop, and I'm not much of a hunter anymore, but I'm born and raised in the South, so I've spent my share of time in the woods. Hunters creep through the woods like Elmer Fudd huntin' wabbits, which is to say not as quietly as we like to think. But something eerie and beautiful happens when we do come to a complete stop.

Eventually, if you stand perfectly still and perfectly quiet long enough, the woods come to life. Even though you thought you were completely alone, the area is suddenly teeming with life. All the creatures that had stopped to watch you have decided that you're not worth watching anymore, and they go back to their regularly scheduled programming.

If you just stop, look, listen, and smell, you eventually get to see the world as it actually is.

Even if you have no plans for putting on the old ghillie suit and traipsing out into the wild, you can benefit from the occasional SLLS break.

Most modern work can be described as hours of tedium interrupted by moments of slightly less monotonous tedium.

But improved focus will lead to improved productivity.

So every once in awhile, reacquaint yourself with the present moment. Try lifting your head from the email. Stop and give the real world a look, listen, and a big ol sniff.

You might be surprised to see, hear, and smell how it actually is.

An SLLS break is perfect to punctuate the end of one Pomodori sessions and the start of another.

Pomodori can get you started. Pomodori can keep you focused. And combined with one more favorite productivity hack that I'm about to show you, they can help you turn actions into habits and turn your whole life around.

I learned that watching Seinfeld.

"TV Guide" says *The Contest* from the fourth season of **Seinfeld** is the best episode of situation comedy. I happen to agree.

In my favorite scene, Kramer leaves Jerry's apartment after he, Jerry, and George notice an attractive woman galavanting around in the buff in an apartment across the street. He returns to the room 53 seconds later, slams a fistful of dollars on the countertop and proclaims "I'm out!"

He is no longer the master of his domain.

After George's mother caught him pleasuring himself with a particularly steamy issue of *Glamour* magazine and he swears off touching himself, the gang, including Elaine, had entered into a group bet, a contest to see who can go the longest without doing the deed. Kramer is first out.

Eventually they all succumb to temptation. Elaine is pushed over the edge by a spin class with JFK Jr., Jerry by a series of frustrating dates, and George by a nurse with a sponge.

Temptation is everywhere.

In the episode, George is the presumed last man standing, but it's Seinfeld himself who is the true master of his domain. And he's helped me become the master of mine.

Comedy pays the bills, but Jerry Seinfeld is more important to me for his eponymous productivity hack: The Seinfeld Technique

The story goes like this. A young comedian approached Seinfeld one day, bemoaning his lack of progress in the comedy world. And Jerry tells him that if he ever wants to get anywhere he's going to have to write better material and explains the simple fact that if you want to write better material, you have to write *more* material. You have to write every day. Practice. Practice. Practice.

The young comedian goes on to list all the standard excuses: I get writer's block. I don't feel creative. I'm waiting for inspiration to strike. I need to be in the right mood to write. I haven't really felt like writing. Yada Yada Yada.

But inspiration doesn't just strike out of the blue. Work doesn't just happen. And more often than not, we don't really feel like doing the things we know we need to be doing more of.

It's not very often that we wake up in the mood to make a ton of cold calls to sales prospects.

Most of the time we don't "feel like" going for a run or going to the gym or eating our veggies, or in the case of the failing comedian, writing new jokes.

Usually we know what the right thing to do is. Having the discipline to do it on a consistent basis is where we struggle.

Another famous Jerry, Coach Jerry West said this: "You can't get much done in life if you only work on the days when you feel good."

The Seinfeld Technique can help you get started on work on days when you don't feel like it and help you build the habit of doing the work every day. Day in and day out.

Seinfeld would buy himself a big year-at-a-glance calendar and a sharpie. And he would sit down to write. And every day he wrote he would draw a giant red X for that day on the calendar. Once he would write for a couple of days in a row, he'd have a streak going. And he'd do everything possible to not break the streak.

It works. And at first glance, it's brilliantly simple.

But the why and the how are where the genius really comes out.

First off, it gamifies your productivity, turning something you dread into something you look forward to.

It's a game, and work made fun gets done.

Marking that big red x on the calendar lights up all the reward and pleasure centers in your head, the same as a Dunkin' Donut in your mouth or a needle in your arm.

And just like Pavlov's dog and the dinner bell, you'll do all you can do to keep the treats coming. Who's a good boy? Who's a good boy?!

In *How To Win Friends and Influence People*, Dale Carnegie tells the story of the president of a steel company who pays a visit to the worst performing steel mill in the company.

Now he could have yelled and screamed and threatened to fire every employee unless they ramped up production and fast. But he didn't.

He could have stood in front of them and appealed in soaring eloquence to their higher nature, patriotism, baseball, hot dogs, apple pie, and momma. But he didn't.

And he could have offered raises, bonuses, trips to Cancun, extra vacation days, oriental massages, and steak dinners if they would just, for the love of God, raise production. He didn't do that either.

What he did do was quietly walk over to the foreman of the day shift, which was just coming to an end, and ask, "How many batches did you guys heat today?"

"Six," says the foreman.

Then the president, one of the richest, most powerful men in America at the time, borrows a pieces of chalk, gets down on the floor and draws a huge number 6 right in the middle of the floor. Gets up and walks out without saying a word.

When the night shift comes in a few minutes later, the first thing they want to know is why there's a giant 6 on the floor. And the day shift guys tell them.

"You won't believe this. The big boss man was in here today in his suit and tie, stove top hat, and monocle glasses asking how many batches we heated today, and then he gets down on his hands and knees and draws the number on the floor. That dude's crazy." (Or whatever the industrial revolution era equivalent of "dude" was.)

Then the night shift gets to work and all night they're staring at that big 6, not wanting to be outdone, so they work a little harder, spend a little less time doing whatever steelworkers did at the turn of the last century to waste time when the bosses weren't looking, and when the day shift comes in the next morning, there on the middle of the mill floor they find a giant number 7.

And it was on.

Soon the mill was cranking out 10 or more batches of steel per shift, doubling production and taking themselves from worst to first in the entire company.

Why?

Because instead of prodding, pandering, or bribing, the big boss man threw down a challenge, offered up a little friendly competition. He made it a game. He made it fun.

And work made fun gets done.

It's the reason behind the entire new fitness tracking industry, the little doodads and doohickeys that track how many steps you take each day, how many calories you burn, how many miles you walk or run. And then, most importantly, posts them on Twitter so you can compare yourself to your friends. A little friendly competition.

It's why car dealerships have gongs and bells and buzzers that sound every time someone makes a sale. And why they have sales boards in the back that show how many cars each and every salesperson has sold so far that month. Not for the bonus money, but for the competition.

It's why there's even such a thing as Klout. So people like me who spend way too much time on the internet can turn all of our pictures of grumpy cats and Zig Ziglar quotes into a little game to see how much we can raise our score and compare it to our friends.

It's why we keep score.

The Seinfeld Technique challenges you to keep score, compete against yourself, and keep the streak alive. Every day, it asks "What's Your Number?"

The Seinfeld Technique uses the science of small wins to create inertia.

It uses inertia to create habits.

And if you can change your habits, you can change your life.

I keep a clipboard on my desk with a spreadsheet of my streaks. The things I try to get done every day, day in and day out. There's about a dozen and they change periodically.

I can unequivocally say this: Jerry Seinfeld has changed my life.

As I sit here and type this, I haven't had a drink in 1,058 days.

I've ran at least a mile every day for the last 267 days.

I meditate every day. Do a plank every day. And spend focused periods of time every day on my business and writing.

So what about you? Are you ready to become the master of your domain?

What daily habit can the Seinfeld Technique help you develop?

What can you do today, tomorrow and everyday thereafter to build a better life?

Most self help experts preach about willpower and motivation, but the truth is your habits and your ability to focus on a task at hand will be what decide your success no matter what kind of improvement you seek.

Willpower is overrated and motivation isn't strong enough.

The Buddha said: "There are only two mistakes one can make along the road to truth; not going all the way, and not starting."

You can use the Pomodoro and Seinfeld techniques to get you started and keep you going. And eventually it becomes habit, a way of life. One day, you may find the thing that had been such a chore brings you your greatest joy.

Like cleaning the pool for instance. I used to hate cleaning the pool. Hated it.

It was frustrating. I was constantly thinking to myself and saying out loud to anyone who would listen. "Why am I the one cleaning the pool? I don't even swim in it!"

I tried everything to get out of cleaning the pool. For a while we had a little robot thingy that was supposed to crawl along the bottom of the pool and keep it clean. It did not, however, work as advertised.

I tried delegating responsibility to my kids. The pool was for them after all (insert eye rolls here). That didn't work out either.

When all else fails, they say, hire a professional. So I did that to. Several to be exact. But then I just spent my time bitching about spending my money. And finding someone reliable, dependable, and qualified turned out to be a much bigger challenge than you might expect.

Honestly, even when I found a decent guy, he wasn't able to keep the pool much cleaner than the robot. My pool is surrounded by trees and fields of grass. In the spring pollen falls from the sky in streaming storms of yellow. Followed by helicopter attacks from the maples. And finally the blinding blizzard of leaves in the fall.

A pool service coming by to skim, brush and chlorinate the pool once a week was doomed to failure no matter how reliable, dependable, and qualified they were.

What the pool needed was consistent, focused attention. There was work that needed to be done.

And the only way to do it is to do it.

The Pomodoro Technique taught me that about half an hour of focused effort will go a long way toward solving most problems in my life and, in the case of keeping the pool clean, it doesn't even take half an hour. All it really takes is about ten minutes a day.

And the willpower to do it every day.

Leaves, dust, and pollen fall in the pool every day.

Birds poop in the pool every day.

Algae grows and colonizes bit by bit, slowly but surely, every day.

The algae doesn't care that the pool guy isn't scheduled to come back until Thursday to chlorinate again.

The leaves don't care if you skimmed the pool yesterday, or that the filter is already clogged. They keep falling.

And the birds keep pooping. Every. Damn. Day.

So the pool needs cleaning. Every. Damn. Day.

The constant struggle to keep the leaves and the pollen and the dust and everything else out of the pool can almost drive you crazy. It's a constant irritation. A raven knock, knock, knocking on your door.

Until you learn to accept the first rule of pool ownership.

There's always going to be a little bird poop in the pool.

And leaves. And pollen. And dust. And insects. And organic matter of all kinds.

You'll never get it all out. And you'll drive yourself crazy trying.

Embrace imperfection.

I've got friend who used to run out of his house screaming and chasing the birds whenever they flew near his pool. Cussing them. Shaking his fists at them every time one dropped a load in his pool. Like his displeasure had any effect at all on their regularity.

When they gotta go, they gotta go.

And all you can do is all you can do.

Brush the pool. Skim the pool. Chlorinate the pool.

Today. Tomorrow. And the day after that.

It's all you can do. And all you can do is enough.

Keep it simple.

I've tried countless sanitizing systems. And different filters. And fancy new chemicals.

And I would spend three or four days a week in line at the pool store standing in line to get the water tested and have them tell me that I needed to buy 10 pounds of such and such chemical to counteract the 12 pounds of such and such chemical that 48 hours ago they told me I needed to bring my such and such levels down to such and such parts per million while maintaining my other such and such level at such and such parts per million.

Holy crap! It's a swimming pool not a chemistry lab.

After years of trial and error I came to the conclusion that I really only needed 3 things.

I needed to keep chlorine in the pool; so I have a little plastic duck (his name is Alfred, by the way) floating around the pool that I keep filled with chlorine tabs. Easy peasy. And I haven't bothered testing the water in years.

I needed to sweep the pool every day to keep the carbon up and floating around where the chlorine could do its job.

And I needed to remove as much organic material as I could.

Over the years they sold me sand filters and fancy cartridge filters and some other filters with names I can't pronounce. And they sold me even fancier systems for cleaning the filters. What I came to realize though, was that the filters were just keeping the crap in my pool. They were one more thing I had to wash, clean and worry about.

Honestly, now I just use coffee filters. I keep a coffee filter in the skimmer and change it daily when I sweep the pool. No muss. No fuss. And a year's supply costs me about $1.97.

Rejoice in the way things are.

I spent years fighting it. Trying to find the easiest, most efficient way to avoid doing the thing that needed to be done. But my resistance only made me miserable and made the job that much harder to do it.

And the funny thing is once I accepted the inevitable, once I gave into that which was required, this horrible, horrible chore became the highlight of my day.

I spent a decade trying to figure out new and more expensive ways to avoid spending 10 minutes a day outside basking in the glorious sunshine, breathing in the good clean Tennessee air and playing in my own personal 20,000 gallon tank of clean, crisp, refreshing water.

I can barely remember what I fought so hard to avoid.

I get the feeling that a lot of things are like that. If we can just learn to put aside our worry, our dread, and our expectations for the future, if we can just learn to block out our regrets, our misremembered nostalgia, and our never-ending what ifs from the past, if we can try living our lives right here, right now in this one glorious moment, we'll find out it's the best of all possible worlds if for no other reason than it's the only world possible.

Rejoice in the way things are. Everything is as it should be.

ACTION STEPS

1) SET THE TIMER. Find the timer app on your phone or just type SET TIMER for 25 minutes in the Google search bar and spend the next 25 minutes doing something you've been putting off: clean your room, clean your desk, cold call sales prospects, do the books, grade some papers. Get busy getting busy and see how much you can get done before the bell tolls.

2) TAKE A BREAK. Stop what you're doing and give this moment, this here and now, your complete undivided attention. Engage all your senses. What do you see? What do you hear? What do you smell?

3) MAKE A LIST. What are some habits that you would like to develop? What's something you think you should do every day, but can't muster up the willpower and motivation to do regularly? Exercise. Write. Eat your veggies. No snacking after 8 pm. Up and at them before 7 am.

4) PICK ONE. You can't concentrate on everything so pick one habit that you want to start today. And start. Draw a big red X on the calendar. That's one in a row. You've started a streak.

5) DON'T BREAK THE STREAK. Now, do it again tomorrow. And the day after that. And the day after that.

6) BRAG ABOUT IT. Send me a tweet to @TerryLancaster and tell me how many days in a row you've got going. #DontBreakTheStreak

For more info on ways to improve your focus and productivity so you can spend more time HERE NOW visit TerryLancaster.com/focus.

Don't Worry About A Thing,
'Cause Every Little Thing Gonna Be Alright.

8. Let It Go

Ob-La-Di. Ob-La-Da.

It was as if there had never been the word "air" and then one day, all anyone could talk about was this new thing called "air" that surrounds us all day every day, that's fundamental to life itself, that we experience with literally every breath we take. In 2013, they even added it to the dictionary with other recently bloomed words like "twerk" and "selfie."

But the word wasn't "air"

It was "FOMO," an acronym for Fear Of Missing Out.

The Oxford Dictionary defines FOMO as:

Anxiety that an exciting or interesting event may currently be happening elsewhere, often aroused by posts seen on a social media website.

Including the social media aspect in the definition might make it a newfangled concept, but the fear of missing out is as pervasive and fundamental to the way we experience the world as ... air.

Sometimes the exciting or interesting event that may currently be happening elsewhere is as close as the neighborhood grocery store at the next checkout line over. The line that always seems to be moving faster than the one you're in.

Sometimes the excitement is as far away as Wall Street where all the money seems to be rushing into small cap stocks, just as you switch to large caps. And in the homegrown S&P 500 stocks just as you reallocate your portfolio to emerging markets.

FOMO is just a high tech way of describing something we've felt all our lives:

The Grass Is Always Greener on the Other Side of the Fence

Except it's not.

And intellectually we know it's not.

But that doesn't make us feel any better when all those people over there are scanning in their groceries, chatting and snickering with the cashier, making snide comments about all us dumb bastards over here in the "slow" line.

And it sure doesn't make us feel any better when we've got an IRA full of emerging markets stock funds that haven't gone anywhere in the last six years while the S&P has tripled.

Fear of missing out isn't really the fear of missing out. It's the fear of choosing poorly. Maybe more accurately it's the fear of feeling like we've chosen poorly.

I can't imagine that I would ever go skydiving. It certainly seems like it would be an adrenaline rush. And I understand all the mumbo jumbo about life beginning at the edge of your comfort zone and overcoming your fears by facing your fears.

But here's the thing: I'm not afraid of crashing into the ground and I'm not afraid of dying.

I am, however, petrified by the idea that I could jump out of a plane, pull the ripcord to no avail, and spend the next 60 seconds plummeting to the earth contemplating the consequences of my bad decision.

"Terry, you are the biggest dumbass in the history of dumbasses. You are about to hit the ground at 120 mph for no better reason than you wanted an adrenaline rush. Meanwhile, all the cool kids are still up there in that perfectly good airplane ... snickering."

That sinking feeling is the price we pay for having the freedom to choose. It's the tyranny of choice.

We think we want more choices. We think options are a pathway to happiness. Happiness is always obtainable as long as we make the right choices.

But that's how they get ya.

Because no matter what you choose, there's always the nagging little voice in the back of your head, in the pit of your stomach, that says "what if."

There's always the road not taken.

We like to say that America is built on the freedom to choose. We get to choose our elected officials. We get to choose which brand of dishwashing detergent to buy. We get to choose where our kids go to college.

But the American economy isn't built on the freedom to choose. The economy is built on the fear of missing out. The green, green grass on the other side of the fence.

The economy is driven by "what if."

That feeling that maybe we made a bad choice keeps us in a constant state of stress and dissatisfaction looking for a slightly better choice to make that feeling go away.

So we hope the next guy we elect isn't going to be as bad as the last one, but he (or she) always is.

We hope the new and improved dishwashing detergent will leave our glasses both streakless and spotless without any extra effort on our part. And we pay ever-increasing tuition for an ever-declining ROI educating our children for jobs that no longer exist, but would now require a master's degree if they did.

FOMO keeps the rats running without ever realizing that the race is just a wheel.

FOMO makes us buy shit we don't need with money we don't have to impress people we don't like.

FOMO makes us do shit we don't want to do on the off chance that someone else might be enjoying themselves doing it.

A few years ago, before I got off the booze, I would spend two or three nights a week closing down the smokiest, diviest, dingiest bar in Nashville with my hockey buddies. We'd sit in there, night after night, week after week, telling the same stories to the same guys who have heard all those stories a million times before. And maybe one night out of a hundred something interesting would happen. Someone new would have a new story. Or someone would get stupid drunk and do something really stupid. No one wants to miss that. So we showed up week after week.

Just in case.

FOMO makes us watch TV shows we don't want to watch so we can have something to talk about while we're sitting around waiting for something interesting to happen.

And maybe that's the scariest thing of all. FOMO is a self-fulfilling prophecy. We're so preoccupied with searching for the next new thing to take away that nagging "what if" feeling that we never get around to enjoying the thing we have now.

Our fear of missing out causes us to miss out.

Let It Go.

All the stuff the cool kids have is just stuff.

And all that green grass on the other side of the fence, it's still just grass.

As the father of three daughters, I have a basement full of the remnants of female childhood: piles and piles of dress-up clothes and costumes, dolls and dollhouses and doll accessories of every conceivable kind (yes Barbie had a Jeep and a Corvette) and most importantly shelves full of Disney movies (on VHS by the way and I haven't seen a working VHS player in about a decade).

And little girls love them some Disney Princesses. The Princesses have to have made Disney more money than the mouse ever dreamed of. One of my daughters is a redhead, and she spent her entire childhood wanting to be Ariel from *The Little Mermaid*, and then along came Merida in *Brave* just to complicate matters.

I would like to say my daughters outgrew all this, and those shelves of dusty VHS tapes in the basement are the only traces Princess envy in the house, but that's not the way it works. I'm not sure little girls ever out grow Disney Princesses, and nothing proves this more than *Frozen*.

Frozen came out a few years ago and was a cultural landslide; suddenly every little girl was in an Elsa costume and you literally could not escape the ubiquitous theme song, *Let It Go*.

Well, I couldn't escape it anyway. My grown-ass daughters played and sang and watched the song on YouTube nonstop. I think one of them had it as a ringtone on their phone. The problem was compounded by the fact that the song was sung by Idina Menzel who had spent several seasons on "Glee," their favorite TV show.

Let It Go! Let It Go!

And this was about the time I was starting to make serious changes in my life.

I quit drinking.

I quit eating for sport and started eating for fuel.

I quit watching the news entirely and cut back dramatically on TV in general.

I let it all go.

And belted out more than a few choruses: *Let It Go! Let It Go!*

I set out to declutter and simplify my life by getting rid of all the stuff I didn't really need which it turns out is almost everything we cling to.

Over the last few years, I've come to the conclusion that human beings really only need seven things, not only to survive, but to thrive. Everything above and beyond those seven is not only optional, it's a distraction, a hindrance for living the life we were born to lead

- *Fresh Air*

- *Sunshine*

- *Clean Water*

- *Real Food*

- *Exercise*

- *Meditation*

- *Human Connection*

We spend half our lives wandering around lost in thought and most of the time what we're thinking about has no bearing on our actual lives.

Let It Go! Let It Go!

We seek out entertainment like it was more important than real food and clean water combined. We may work 40 hours a week, but we spend almost that much time parked in front of the TV screen - on average 35 hours a week.

And of the money we earn from that 40-hour week, most of us spend as much or more of it on entertainment than we do on groceries.

But every hour you spend in front of a TV screen takes another 22 minutes off your life because of inactivity and snacking according to the British Journal of Sports Medicine.

Hell, watching TV is more dangerous than smoking according to *The New York Times*.

Every cigarette you smoke only gets you out of the old age home 11 minutes faster. If you're bound and determined to die young and leave a bountiful corpse … kick back and enjoy some tube.

That's 22 minutes you lose in addition to the hour of your life that you wasted watching mindless drivel.

That hour you spent watching Honey Boo Boo … you're not getting that back.

And the human need for narrative is infinitely more addictive than nicotine could ever be. What other possible explanation could there be for Honey Boo Boo to even exist?

Your brain is the most complex network in the known universe, trillions of synapses linked for just one reason: To take the tidal wave of information that our senses bring in from the world around us, the infinite set of data points that we gather each moment, filter out the redundancy and noise, and weave it all together in a nice little simple narrative that we like to call reality.

If cigarettes are nothing more than a nicotine delivery device, your television is nothing more than a ready made instant reality delivery system. We get a nice story that makes us laugh, smile, cry, and sometimes scream without all the messy hassle of actually living a life.

Roughly 100,000 years ago, humans gathered around the campfires in the evening. They gathered for the warmth of the fire, for the companionship and protection of the group, and most of all, for the stories, for the narratives that helped them make sense of the world, created their paradigms and shaped their reality.

They gathered for the lies we tell ourselves about ourselves.

And that's why we still gather.

That's why we watch the crap they put on TV today. The addiction is wired in.

But we've got to kick the habit.

The sole purpose of modern commercial television is to make your life seem disappointing and sell you shit to ease the pain.

Opt out.

Watching even a little less TV frees up the time you need for the true passions in your life.

It gives you the time you say you don't have to do the things you need to do to give yourself the life you deserve.

Spend less time watching the tube and more time exercising, playing, talking to your family and your friends. More time working harder to make your dreams come true.

Quit comparing your life to the make-believe lives you see on your TV.

Turn off the TV and get busy leading a life, a real life, so interesting, so amazing that people want to watch you play.

Life is not a spectator sport. Play more. Watch less.

We get all dressed up in our favorites team's jerseys and worship at the altar of big time college and pro sports from the comfort of our living room. We talk about our favorite sports. We learn all the stats and argue ad infinitum about the minutia of offense and defense. But we don't go outside and play.

I've seen grown in men in fist fights over college football. And not even alumni, we're talking about people who have never set foot on a college's campus … fighting about some shit they saw on TV.

I'm a little uncomfortable with the whole concept of spectator sports. Spectator sports is an oxymoron like governmental efficiency and well-behaved children.

The truth of the matter is that spectator sports is pornography.

Not lock the office door, turn down the volume, and clear the browser history pornography, but pornographic in the sense that we've idealized and objectified athletes in the same way we've idealized and objectified solid granite counter tops, exotic sports cars ... and Honey Boo Boo.

As a culture, we like to watch.

We crave heroes to worship, and we lift athletes up as shining examples of what you can do if you put your mind, your heart, and your back into it.

But we've taken their hard work and accomplishment and turned it into an excuse to sit around a 60-inch TV screen eating chips and drinking light beer.

The blood and grass stains on their uniforms do not equate with the Cheetos stains on our fingers.

Our admiration suffocates our participation. We'd rather watch than play.

People who know how much I love playing hockey will often ask me why I don't go to more NHL games and I always tell them the same thing:

"They don't come watch me play. Why should I go watch them?"

It drives me crazy every year on Super Bowl Sunday when our regular Sunday night hockey league is cancelled so everyone can stay home and *watch* a football game. I don't get it.

Football is the perfect content to trick us into watching more TV because since almost nothing happens it requires very little attention and leaves lots of time to slip in the commercials and promotional announcements.

In fact, commercial minutes outnumber football minutes by almost 5 to 1!

An average football broadcast lasts about three hours from pregame commentary to the post game interviews. You even get a half time show. But for the vast majority of those three hours nothing happens. There's no there, there.

The last time I tried attending a pro football game, I actually fell asleep. Seriously. Nothing happens.

In the average three hour broadcast there's actually about 12 minutes of play going on. Snap to whistle.

Now the first time I read that, I didn't believe. It doesn't even make sense. Why would millions of people spend three hours to watch 54 minutes of commercials (18 minutes an hour) and 12 minutes of football? But it's true, I say. It's true!

I recorded a game on my DVR once and fast forwarded through all the huddles and the replays and the commercials and the in-depth analysis, and yes, I even fast-forwarded through the cheerleaders. I took about 12 minutes to watch the game.

If you do the math, it works out that the actual playing time in a Hall of Fame football career is about 20 hours.

Legends are made. Fortunes are built. Legacies created. All based on one good solid part-time work week.

The genius of football is what it makes us think. How it makes us feel.

Football sprinkles crazy dust in our brain and makes us think amazing, intricate complicated things are going on when hardly anything happens at all.

Football makes us think we're all jocks because we spend countless hours a week watching TV, drinking beer, and eating nachos. And believe me, if watching TV, drinking beer, and eating nachos were an Olympic event, America would win hands down. We own that shit.

Management consultants will tell you to learn the difference between your areas of concern and your areas of influence. Then concentrate your energies on things that you can affect.

Dale Carnegie tells us not to worry about things we can't control.

And The Serenity Prayer asks for serenity to accept the things we cannot change, the courage to change the things we can and the wisdom to know the difference.

No matter how many times you wear your favorite player's jersey inside out … No matter how loudly you yell at the screen … No matter how many times you call the idiot jerk on the sports talk show to set him straight … You have zero power to control, affect, or influence the sports you're watching on the tube. Zero.

Your area of influence is what happens in the area right around you. With the people right around you. Your family. Your friends. Your business associates.

To the extent that watching sports can help you form a bond or sense of community with them, I'm all for it.

But you know what's better for building bonds and community than watching other people do stuff? Actually getting off your ass and doing stuff yourself.

Do stuff with the people you love. Do stuff with the people you work with. Do stuff with people you want to work with.

Turn off the TV and get in the game.

Politics is even worse. It's all just a storyline for the soap opera that we call the evening news. We watch the news and documentaries and educational TV telling ourselves we need to stay informed and current. What we're really doing is confirming our own biases and gathering intel for our next big argument with our damn know-it-all Democrat brother-in-law.

But our health, happiness, and prosperity have almost nothing to do with who's in the White House and almost everything to do with who's in our house.

Our nation's President there at the White House surrounded by all the pomp and pageantry of the state ... he's just some guy on TV in a nice suit.

He makes us feel better or he gives us something to hate, but either way, it's a damn good story.

For a long, long time, politics was kinda my thing. I thought I was smarter than everyone else and if everyone else would just agree with me and elect other people who agreed with me, we could make the world a better place.

I was a rabid ditto-head who planned my day around listening to Rush Limbaugh's latest rants. I would argue trickle-down economics with anyone who remotely seemed interested (and more than a few who didn't). And then there was my little shrine to Reagan ... jelly beans, candles, and ammunition. Man, I sure did love Ronnie.

I believed in peace through superior firepower. Prosperity through deregulation. And better government through an informed populace.

Unfortunately, I was wrong. At least about the last part anyway.

Better governments and informed populations are both urban legends like Bigfoot, the alligator in the New York sewers, and low sodium bacon that actually tastes like bacon.

I haven't voted in years, and I don't argue about politics, ever.

Every political argument, every political spin master's pontification, every other freaking commercial on TV during an election year can be summed up in 14 words:

"My lying sack of shit is better than your lying sack of shit ... Nah!"

I can't really put a finger on the exact moment I quit caring. I guess George the First's Read My Lips moment lead me to the Lying Sack of Shit epiphany.

But Bill Clinton ... Bill Clinton is the one that really did me in. I thought Clinton was one of the Four Horsemen of the Apocalypse. I was convinced he was a deep-cover Soviet spy and his election would be the downfall of the capitalist system. In an ironic twist of fate, it took a Republican to do that.

Turns out Bill Clinton was just a bright redneck from the Deep South with a good speaking voice and a weakness for plus-sized junior college dropouts ... What's not to like about that?

I've tried over the years to figure out why people with more money than they know what to do with or really, really smart people who could make lots of money elsewhere spends so much time, energy, and money running for political office.

I mean you've got to kiss a lot of ass just to get elected dog catcher; I don't even want to think what you've got to kiss to get elected president.

Which led to the formation of my first rule of politics:

Anyone who desires political office and is willing to do what it takes to get elected is therefore, by definition, morally unfit for the job.

So I don't know who that leaves to run things, but whatever happens, you can't blame me. I didn't vote for any of 'em.

And I don't watch them on TV.

Spectator sports may be pretty good at tricking us into watching more TV. But politics and the news in general not only trick us into wasting our lives in front of the tube, they have somehow convinced us that it's our moral and civic responsibility. That we have a duty to stay informed and watch more commercials.

So we're ravenous for more information. We don't seem to care if it is accurate, intelligent, or useful. We just want more. We want to be INFORMED!

But that's the thing. By definition if it's inaccurate, unintelligent and useless, it isn't information, it's noise. And that's what the news is. It's noise.

Now it would be easy for me to blame this on the 24-hour news cycle, citizen journalism via Twitter, and our entire everything we want, right now on demand, fast food, quick buck culture, but the truth is the news has always just been noise, although not in the loud cover-your-eardrums sense of the word.

Of course, most everything on TV is noisy like that, too.

But news is noise in the information theory sense of the word: random, meaningless, irrelevant data. Information theorists use the signal-to-noise ratio to discuss the balance between useful information and irrelevant data.

The news is irrelevant, and always has been.

In Journalism 101, they teach the standard definition of news. If the dog bites the man, that's not news. It happens thousands of times a day. It's commonplace. But if the man bites the dog, that's news. And it's news precisely because it's out of the ordinary. If men were biting dogs by the thousands, you wouldn't need a reporter to tell you about it.

It's irrelevant to your life. It's a sideshow. An oddity. It provides no other benefit to you other than to satisfy your morbid curiosity and innate voyeurism.

If the news being irrelevant was its worst side-effect, it might be ok. But it's not.

The news skews your view of the world.

The news has an inherent bias towards big splashy events like bombings and terrorists attacks. But this bias and the constant beating of the drum leads us to overestimate the danger from such events.

A few years ago, the media declared the summer of the shark because of all the shark attacks off America's coastlines. Virtually every newscast led with a reporter standing on a beach, Geraldo Riviera style, detailing another atrocity. But at summer's end, the statisticians went to work and the accurate, intelligent useful information was that shark attacks, and deaths were BELOW average for the year. The summer of the shark was a media invention.

And it leads us to dramatically *underestimate* the danger from such mundane, non-newsworthy topics as sitting in front of our TV's 5 hours a day, drinking sugar water, and eating over-processed, edible food-like substances in eye catching packages.

The news is biased.

Back to Journalism 101, they talk a lot about fair, balanced, and unbiased coverage. Well, first of all, there's no such thing as fair, but that's an entirely different rant. Every human being has biases, most of which we aren't even aware of, you know, because we're biased. Every story a reporter covers, every decision a news director makes, every "fact" an editor accepts as truth is a function of their own bias. The news is biased, at its best.

At its worst, the news is propaganda.

We love to boast about our free press and the first amendment while condemning the state-controlled media in other less-evolved cultures. Our media may jump through a few more hurdles to give the appearance of free, fair, and balanced, but make no mistake, every report you see on the news, every article you read is there because it's in someone's economic or political interest for it to be there. Spin doctors, PR gurus, and publicists are pulling the strings of the media, the same way that lobbyists and fundraisers are pulling the strings of the politicians.

They don't even try to hide it. The media corporations are the some of the largest corporations in the world. And corporations exist for only one reason: to make a profit.

The news is marketing. Pure and simple.

It's a shiny package to wrap around the advertising. It's sole purpose is to attract your attention and keep it long enough to rent out to the highest bidder. Not that there's anything wrong with that. I sell ads for a living. But when one of my big loud-ass car commercials comes on TV, at least you know it's an ad. The news is like product placement in your favorite TV show. It makes you think all the cool kids are drinking Vitamin Water, and you don't even know you just got sold.

But the absolutely, positively worst thing about the news is that it is a giant, useless, black hole of time suck.

They've convinced you that you need to stay up to date on current affairs, that you need to be in the know so you'll watch hours of their drivel every day. Between the local news at 6 and 10, the national news, your Facebook and Twitter feed, God forbid an actual newspaper or news magazine, and then the countless dinner conversations about the news that you get sucked into, it's easy to waste two even three hours a day on the "news."

And the news ain't the news.

That's a full day of every week, wasted, keeping up with things that have absolutely no bearing on your life.

I understand the attraction. I've got a degree in journalism and I am a reformed news junkie, but junkie is the correct word. The news is a drug that never satisfies your thirst for knowledge. It only scratches the itch and leaves you wanting more.

I honestly couldn't tell you the last time I watched a newscast. I've opted out.

Block out the noise so you can hear the signal.

Turn off the TV. Put down the remote. And get busy leading a life worth reporting.

You're not missing out on anything.

Let It Go! Let It Go!

ACTION STEPS

1) TURN OFF THE TV. See if you can make it through today without turning on the TV at all. Just one day. No news. No sitcoms. No SportsCenter. If you wake up tomorrow and the world has not come crashing down around you, try it again. Two days in a row is a streak #DontBreakTheStreak

2) TURN THE OTHER CHEEK. Somewhere today, either in the real world or on the Facebook, someone is going to say something about religion, or politics, or your favorite team that just right royally pisses you off. Every fiber of your being will want to correct, argue, inform, or otherwise straighten them out. Don't do it. Even if it's all in good fun, even if you couch your response with a smiley face emoticon. Just walk away.

Let It Go. Let It Go.

3) THROW SOMETHING AWAY. You've got something in your house that you bought once upon a time because it was supposed to be the best thing since sliced bread, because you're friends were buying one and you just had to have it, because it looked so damn useful in all the ads. But it was not the best thing since sliced bread. It was not useful at all and you haven't touched it for years. Throw it out and try to remember that the next time you just have to have some new gadget.

4) HYDRATE. Just for today, don't drink anything but plain water. Clean, crisp, refreshing, glorious water. Not because you're trying to cut out calories. Not for your diet or health. But just to prove that you don't need anything else. All the sweeteners and flavors and packaging that get pushed on you all day, every day are just trying to complicate your mind. Drinking water today can help convince your mind that what you need and what the world tells you should want have very little to do with each other.

5) GO SHOPPING. Head down to the local supermarket and take a look around. There will 40 to 50 thousand different items stocking the shelves and lining the aisles. All in multicolored packages competing for your attention. Giving you unlimited choices. Now remind yourself that 80% of those different items are produced by just 10 companies. Your choices are illusions.

6) TURN THE TV BACK ON. Take a look at the channel listings. I've personally got about a thousand channels. 24 hours a day. Seven days a week. Politics. News. Reality TV. Sports. I've got everything I could ever want to watch and a whole lot of stuff, I'd never consider watching. I've got a channel that offers relaxation videos for my pets, and I don't have any pets! Now remind yourself that 90% of all of those TV programs are controlled by 6 corporations. Your choices are illusions.

7) GO OUTSIDE AND PLAY. Take your kids for a walk. Have a game of catch. Grow a lumberjack beard and join the local Adult Kickball league with all the other hipsters. You don't have to be a 20-year-old star athlete to enjoy sports. Go play.

For more info on how letting go can improve your life visit TerryLancaster.com/letitgo.

Opportunities Emerge From Connections.

9. Connect Widely

The Sum Is Greater Than The Parts.

A physics professor walks into a bar near campus every afternoon and orders two frosty cold lagers.

He drinks one down and offers the other to the empty barstool next to him. Then he leaves. Everyday.

After weeks of this, the bartender finally asks him, what's up with that?

The professor explains that quantum mechanics has proven that trillions upon trillions of sub atomic particles are popping into and out of existence trillions of times a second and that it's entirely within the realm of scientific possibility for a kind, beautiful woman to spontaneously appear on the bar stool next to him, accept the drink he has bought for her, fall in love with him, and they will live happily ever after.

"Well, Doc," says the bartender. I don't understand quantum physics, but this bar is jam packed full of beautiful women every day. Why don't you offer one of them a drink and talk to her? Maybe you'll hit it off."

"Yeah right," the professor replies. "What are the odds of that?"

The professor was right, of course, at least about the first part.

The universe is a swirling soup of uncertainty and possibility.

Particles really do appear out of nothingness ... like magic. And there's no valid scientific reason why trillions of particles couldn't spontaneously appear in the form of a charming co-ed. In fact not only could it happen, eventually, given an infinite amount of time, it will happen. Eventually.

Unfortunately our introverted professor doesn't have that kind of time.

The odds against it happening while he waits are astronomically large, bordering on impossibility, but just not quite.

And yet he has more confidence in that happening than in his ability to initiate an honest, human connection with a real live person who has already materialized right there in the bar.

I've got another joke for you.

An elderly gentleman is sitting on his front porch watching it rain when the police drive by to warn him that the area is flooding and he needs to evacuate immediately.

"No thanks," he says. "I have faith the Lord will save me."

Later that evening, he's still sitting on the front porch and the floodwaters have reached his feet and his front door.

The police come by again, this time in a rescue boat and implore him one more time to evacuate for his own safety.

"No thanks," he repeats. "I have faith the Lord will save me."

By the next morning the waters have reached the top of his house and he's huddled out on the roof when the National Guard helicopters come by and drop down a rope ladder to whirl him away to safety.

Again, he refuses their aid.

The waters rise and the man is washed away to his death.

At the Pearly Gates of heaven, he confronts Saint Peter.

"I've been a man of the Lord my entire life. Why did he forsake me? Why did he forget about me in my hour of need."

"Nobody forgot about you, man," Saint Peter tells him.

"We sent a police car, a boat, and a helicopter. What on God's green Earth were you waiting for?"

It seems the Lord, and apparently quantum mechanics, help those who help themselves.

Yes, miracles happen every day.

But mostly they're waiting on you to get the ball rolling.

Connectivity overcomes uncertainty.

Quantum mechanics show us that matter exists at all because we observe it. Because we've made a connection with it.

The particles in the shape of charming young coeds in the off campus bar remain in that shape because they're connected with each other and with the young men who are doing the observing.

The elderly gentleman could have saved himself at any point simply by extending his hand to another and making the connection.

Anything can happen. Anything happens all the time.

But mostly it happens because someone made it happen. Mostly with the help of others.

What's going on in your life, right now, that you're praying about, hoping for, wishing for, waiting for, lighting candles for and building dream boards to help you visualize?

If you wish hard enough, eventually it will happen. The laws of physics demand it.

But whatever it is, it will happen a lot quicker if you actually get up, connect with someone, and do something about it.

Opportunities emerge from connections.

The concept of emergence appears in many areas of science.

Emergence is basically when a network, a group, or a system exhibits properties that are not readily apparent in any of the individual elements that make up the group.

Basically when the whole is greater than the sum of the parts.

Trillions and trillions of proteins and acids swirled around the primordial ocean and formed themselves into living micro-organisms where no living beings had existed before.

Trillions and trillions of neurons in the human brain combined and connected and communicate until one day consciousness appeared. A fully self-aware being capable of symbolism and imagination where no such thing had ever existed before.

The sum is greater than the parts.

The connections created a network and the network created something entirely new.

Humans have been creating networks since the dawn of time. We formed tribes that allowed us to hunt and feed on larger, more dangerous animals.

We formed villages that allowed us to master the seasons and the soil at the dawn of the agricultural revolution.

The villages connected and grew into empires with religions and government and armies that have changed the face of the earth and carried us to the moon and back.

Connections are what make humans human. We're social animals.

And in almost every area of your life, your success will largely be determined, not by how smart you are, not by how hard your work, not by how attractive you are, but by your connections.

Dale Carnegie literally wrote the book for self-improvement and social climbing, *How To Win Friends And Influence People*. His manifesto says that only about 15% of most people's financial and career success is due to technical expertise or talent. Even in technical fields, the other 85% depends on social factors like personality, and the ability to lead and motivate others.

Your success depends on your ability to form connections.

Human engineering.

We've all hear the old adage: It's not what you know. It's who you know.

And a lot of us 99%ers use that as an excuse to explain away our failures. We weren't born with a silver spoon in our mouth, how can we be expected to keep up with those who were?

But that's really an opportunity in disguise. An opportunity to connect.

Connections are useless, even to those born into luxury, comfort, and prestige if they're never put to use.

President George H. W. Bush, the poster boy for wealth and privilege, was evangelical about writing thank you notes, starting when he was a small town politician in Texas and continuing through his days in the White House, when he would send dozens of thank you notes a day to everyone from the guy who carried his luggage to other world leaders.

All people, great and small, appreciate being appreciated.

And President George the First used that simple human fact to build and strengthen his personal network, a network that lifted him to the most powerful office in the world for one single term.

But President Bush lost his bid for a second term in office to a politician with much less lofty roots.

Bill Clinton was born in a backwater Arkansas town. The son of a travelling salesman who died before he was born, he was raised by an alcoholic and abusive stepfather.

If he was counting only on people he knew, he wasn't going far.

Here's the flip side of the coin about the old saying. It's absolutely true that it's not what you know, it's who you know. But the thing is: You can always get to know more people.

As a young man, Bill Clinton may not have known the right people, but he knew this:

You have to build your network before you need your network.

Even as 22-year-old grad student at Oxford, Clinton was a master networker. At parties he would be introduced to other students and commence to learning everything he could about them. Who they were. Where they were from. Where they were going and what they were going to do. And he wrote the answers down.

If they asked why he was writing all this down, he would tell them flat out, "I'm going to run to be the Governor of Arkansas when I get back, and I'm keeping track of everyone I meet."

Bill Clinton had a little notebook. George H. W. Bush had thank you notes. Both became the most powerful men in the world.

But you have something better than that. More powerful than any silver spoon could ever be. You may even be looking at it right now.

Your mobile phone.

The mobile phone, and the networks it connects to, are the greatest mechanisms ever created, ever even imagined for making connections, building relationships, for distributing information ... for telling stories. For Telling Your Story.

Your life is the story you tell the world. It's the song you sing.

And your cellphone is the most powerful microphone ever invented.

It's like Gutenberg's Printing Press to the infinite power.

I've been carrying around a practically worthless journalism degree for decades, and now, for the first time in my life, the world has changed in such a way that a journalism degree is actually worthwhile. Well, maybe not the degree itself, but the ability to connect, create, and distribute content is probably the most valuable skill in today's economy.

Call it the Tao of Google.

The newspapers I was trained to go to work for are either out of business, damn near out of business, or hanging on by the tiniest strip of border tape leftover from a bygone era. Google now makes more profit than all the newspapers in America ... combined.

It's Google's world, and we're just 7 billion monkeys banging away on 7 billion typewriters feeding the monster.

And increasingly, Google is relying on social media signals to determine which monkey's meanderings get seen in search results, too. Google craves content. It feeds on your stories.

Everyone with a computer or a mobile phone now has the power to create and distribute content just as effectively as *The New York Times* and *The Wall Street Journal*, just as effectively as ABC, NBC, and all the rest of them.

More so, actually. People spend over 25% of their online time surfing social media compared to about 3% of their time watching or reading news (about the same amount they spend on porn).

Depression era gangster Willie Sutton, the original Slick Willie, is often quoted as saying that he robbed banks "because that's where the money is."

Well today, the money is online and on social media.

Two out of three Americans use social media. Forty percent of Americans use social media EVERY DAY. And people who use social media spend an average of two-and-a-half hours per day tweeting, pinning, and liking pictures of grumpy cats.

Back in the days before Al Gore invented the internet there was a saying, "Perception is reality."

Here's another one: "You never get a second chance to make a first impression."

And for the trifecta: "Clothes make the man."

The meaning is clear, and as anyone in marketing will tell you: Packaging Matters!

Twenty years ago which navy blue suit you wore to the local Rotary Club meeting played a large role in what the community thought of you. Who they thought you were.

In today's world you are who Google says you are.

Go ahead. Google yourself. Who does Google say you are? Does Google even know you exist?

If Google can't find you, how in the world do you expect anyone else to?

Ten years or so ago, I had a client who ended up changing employers and wanted to use my service at his new car dealership. He remembered my name, but he couldn't remember the name of my company. And he couldn't find me by name on the interwebs. I lost a couple of years of revenue before we finally were able to get back in touch and I swore that would never happen again.

That was the day I registered the domain name TerryLancaster.com and began creating content to create myself.

Today when I lock the office door, turn down the lights, and Google myself, I generally occupy eight or nine of the 10 listings on the first page.

Google says I'm the VP of Making Sh!t Happen. Google says I'm a speaker, author, and entrepreneur.

Google tells the world who I am. And I tell Google by creating the content it craves.

And Facebook. And Twitter. And LinkedIn. And Pinterest. And Instagram.

I've even got a Myspace page somewhere.

I've got friends in the car business making well into six figures a year selling cars, because they've stepped out onto a limb, creating content, sharing it widely, and becoming a known figure in their local community.

And I've got other friends who have bought their salespeople iPads, sent them through social media training, and encouraged them to create their own personal brand, their own business within a business. A scant two out of 10 might get started. Two out of a 100 might keep at it. Some don't want to put in the work. And some are worried about their privacy and want to remain anonymous online. I guess they're bashful.

But in the immortal words of Zig Ziglar--Bashful salespeople have skinny children.

Once I got serious about building my social network, once I decided that I was the brand, I strengthened my relationships with existing customers. Every day I'm on the phone with clients from Moose Jaw, Saskatchewan to Hog Waller, Alabama, and at least once a day, one of them asks me about something going on in my real life that they read on social media.

"How you likin' that 72 degrees in Nashville?"

"How's your dad doing?"

"You really do naked yoga?"

Now we've got something to talk about besides business. That makes us friends. And friends like to buy from friends.

I've also picked up new customers, been recruited for a couple of six-figure jobs that I never would have known about had I not been engaged on social media and been invited to speak at major conventions.

I would have never had the opportunity to write this book, if I hadn't built a social platform to speak from.

And the truth is as I sit here writing the book, I don't have any idea if anyone besides me and my mother will ever actually read this, and I'm only 80% sure about her.

Twenty-one-year-old Terry could have told you exactly what was going to happen, how many copies of the book would sell, and have a timeline in place for writing my second book. Fifty-one-year-old Terry has lost his desire and his interest for predicting the future.

But I'm planning my work and working my plan, doing all the things that I need to do. I'm perfectly willing to admit that I don't know what's going to happen. I'm OK with that.

But I've created the content and made the connections. As I go out and talk about the book and promote the book, I'll make more connections. And those connections will have connections. And out of those connections opportunities will arise.

Maybe Oprah will come out of retirement with a prime time network television special about the idea of building a better life one better decision at a time. Maybe the book will be a spectacular flop, and I will realize that I need to concentrate my efforts and energies on other areas of my life. Maybe I'll reach just one person with the right message at the right time, help them turn their life around. Maybe they'll send me a nice thank you card; I'd like that.

All of those possibilities are perfectly acceptable, and none of them would have ever happened if I hadn't taken a chance, put myself out there, told my story and connected with the world.

Now I know what some of you are saying.

I'm not a salesperson. I'm not writing a book. How does any of this connection stuff apply to me?

Well here's the truth. Everybody's selling something. You may not work on commission and your business card may not say you're a SALESPERSON, but you are a SALESPERSON.

If you need a better job to make more money and provide a better life for your family, you're a salesperson selling yourself to prospective employers--and you need a better network to help yourself get hired.

If you're lonely and looking for a companion to walk through this life with, looking for a witness to your life, you're a salesperson selling yourself to prospective companions and spouses, and you need a better network to find the right mate.

And sometimes it's not about building a new network or finding new connections. Sometimes it's about strengthening the network we already have. Solidifying our current connections.

If you're married and fighting to stay in the 50% of marriages that don't get divorced, you're a salesperson. Actually in that case you would be called a Major Account Manager and your entire job is keeping one very big customer happy. It's still sales.

Some people say that online connections don't count. That the friends you make on social media aren't your real friends. But I know that that's not true. One third of all new marriages begin with an online relationship.

The internet, email, and social media have revolutionized the way relationships are formed and nurtured. These tools leverage your communications and give you an opportunity to connect with many, many times more people than was ever even imaginable just a few short years ago.

But the dynamics of forming a human bond haven't changed.

My first job out of college was selling radio ads for a station in Tupelo, Mississippi, and my first Sales Manager was a man named Russ Wilson. Russ was a big proponent of community service. He was in the Kiwanis and the Rotary and the Lions clubs. That's where his friends were, and that's where he did business.

He taught me that you have to connect, you have to put yourself out there, you have to engage, and you have to make friends, but you have to be doing it for the right reasons.

You have to be of service and you have to be of value, because if you're just looking to make a sale, then you're not looking for a friend, you're looking for a customer. And people know the difference.

Whether it's over bad chicken at the Civitan Luncheon Club or in your Twitter stream, people know the difference.

The station's General Manager was man named Nick Martin. Nick was my personal hero and was everything I aspired to me. And he couldn't have been more different from Russ if he tried. Except for one all-important characteristic: Like Russ, he was who he was, all day, every day, and apologized to no one for it.

Nick played golf like it was his full time job, and when he wasn't playing golf he was hanging out at the country club for lunch, and when he wasn't hanging out at the club for lunch he was hanging out at the bar after work for drinks. To 21-year-old Terry, that looked like a pretty sweet gig.

Here's the thing, though: he got deals done. I rarely saw him type a sales proposal or even go on a sales call, but he was the station's top salesperson every month.

Turns out that most of the time that he was golfing and lunching and drinking, he was golfing and lunching and drinking with the local Budweiser distributor, the local Pepsi distributor, a car dealer or two and a handful of other major clients that brought in a whole lot more revenue than the fireworks stands and hair salons they were sending me out to call on.

I learned my first rule of sales then: Be their best friend.

Hang out. Talk. Chat. Drink. Play some golf. Wish 'em a happy birthday. You know, be friends.

Most of selling isn't about sales. Most of selling is about building

relationships. And that's exactly what social media can help you do: build relationships.

Social media consultant Ted Rubin says that the primary yardstick of social media isn't ROI (return on investment), but RonR (return on relationship).

By concentrating on building the relationship, you put yourself in a position to get the deal done when it's time to do the deal.

If the General Manager of that small town radio station had wandered out onto the golf course with a briefcase full of pie charts and spec spots, those good ol' boys wouldn't have given him the time of day; but he set out to make friends first.

I started using social media mainly to find out who got fat and bald from high school, but I quickly found out that this social media stuff is pretty useful when it comes to making friends with one very valuable benefit: they buy shit from me.

Friends buy from friends, and that's the way it's always been.

Back when I was working at that small town radio station, driving around the back roads of Mississippi, I often had a cassette tape playing in my car; *The Strangest Secret* by Earl Nightingale.

The Strangest Secret was recorded in 1956 and became the first spoken word recording to ever sell a million copies and receive a Gold Record. The tape can be summed up in six words: We Become What We Think About.

It says so in the bible; As Ye Sow, So Shall Ye Reap.

Many, many years late I saw the movie *The Secret,* which presented the same idea--what has come to be known now as The Law Of Attraction.

Now I've said before, I'm a little skeptical of all the gurus telling us to burn candles and spend all day staring at dream boards filled with yachts and exotic sports cars. But the Law of Attraction is scientific fact and presents itself across the universe in myriad ways.

Like attracts like.

Gravity is the Law of Attraction at work. Matter attracts matter and grows into bigger chunks of matter attracting more matter.

In economics, the rich get richer.

And nowhere is the Law of Attraction more pronounced than in Network Theory, the study of how connections are formed and strengthened to grow into networks.

As connections form, some connecting points will naturally acquire a greater number of connections, which then enable them to acquire even more connections at an ever increasing pace. In Network Theory, The Law of Attraction is called Power Law and the highly connected points are called Super Nodes or Super Connectors. And once they reach a tipping point, they form new connections exponentially. A chart of their newly formed connections takes off like the curve on a hockey stick once they reach critical mass.

The rich get richer.

Like attracts like.

But somewhere along the idea, we got the idea that human connections and networks were somehow different. We decided that opposites attract. Male/Female. Positive/Negative. Yin/Yang.

That's not the way it works. Most relationships are formed among remarkably similar people with similar educations, similar socioeconomic backgrounds, and similar religious beliefs.

And similar dispositions.

There's a scene in one of my all-time favorite TV shows, *Justified*, where US Marshall Raylan Givens is driving a prisoner across Harlan County, and the prisoner is recounting his sad tale of woe. How everyone is out to get him. How he never had a chance. The odds are stacked against him.

I call it the losers war cry: It's Not My Fault.

After a few minutes of listening to the bitching and moaning, Raylan gives a little tug on his ten gallon hat and says,

"If you meet an asshole in the morning, well, you met an asshole. But if you run into assholes all day long, maybe you're the asshole."

Like attracts like.

It's easy to get caught up in the numbers, especially on social media. How many friends do I have? How many followers? How many likes did I get? How many shares?

But how many connections you have is not nearly important as how good the connections are. Whether it's digital or real life, concentrate on making your connections honest--on making them sincere human connections.

If you're trying to build a better network, you have to start by being a better person.

Not being an asshole is a great start.

Your grandmother told you if you didn't have something nice to say, don't say anything at all.

Grandma was a freakin' genius!

But the vast majority of the world is under the impression that every thought that pops into their head needs to be shared with the world. It doesn't.

I've got a few friends who have to close their Facebook accounts down every few months because of all the arguing and negativity. The truth is Facebook only shows you what it thinks you want to see. Your Facebook feed is a pretty accurate reflection of your personality.

Just be nice.

Seriously, the greatest benefit to me of meditation is that I can recognize when thoughts cross my brain, accept them for what they are, and not feel the need to roll down my window, scream, and flip the bird to the douchebag in the BMW who just cut me off in traffic. I don't feel the need to go home and write a rant on my Facebook page about how all BMW drivers are douchebags.

The world doesn't need to know the full list of things that piss you off.

If you hate your job, hate your wife, hate your kids, and hate your life, maybe you want to keep that little bit of sunshine to yourself. Positivity creates engagement. Debby Downer goes to the prom alone.

Remember, you have to build your network before you need your network.

You need to build a network filled with positive, kind, successful, decent human beings.

And the only possible way to attract positive, kind, successful, decent human beings into your life is to be one yourself.

I had someone ask me once how they could get more Twitter followers, and I know they were looking for some super secret, magic bullet type answer. We're always looking for a magic bullet.

But what I told them was this: Follow interesting people, be interested in the things they say, and say interesting things.

It's really that simple, whether you're on Twitter, at the after-work networking event, or at your in-laws for Thanksgiving dinner.

Most conversations aren't really conversations, they're just two people each waiting for their turn to talk.

Put the phone down when you're talking to each other. Be here now.

Focus your full attention on the people in your life whether it's your biggest customer or the cashier at the corner convenience market. Make each interaction a genuine human interaction, with a smile, eye contact, and a couple of please and thank yous thrown in for good measure. The opportunities that begin to flow from those connections will surprise you.

All our lives, we've heard about answering the door when opportunity knocks. Well, I'm here to tell you now, opportunity doesn't knock. Opportunity is not going to come looking for you.

Opportunities only come attached to other people. I honestly can't think of any other kind.

If you want more opportunities to come knocking, invite more people. They'll bring the opportunities with them.

ACTION STEPS

1) PLEASE BE MY FRIEND. Thank You It's a beautiful day in the neighborhood. A beautiful day for a neighbor; would you be mine? Please connect with me on social media and let me help you grow your network and create new opportunities. You can find all my profiles at TerryLancaster.com/contact.

2) SAY THANK YOU. I hope by now, this far into the book, you're on board with the whole Thank You Note thing. But I'm going to give it one more push anyway. Send a thank you note to someone who has done something nice for you today. Gary Vaynerchuk says we now live in the Thank You Economy. Start spreading some appreciation. People like that.

3) STRIKE UP A CONVERSATION. Talk to a stranger on the street. Make eye contact with a cashier and ask them how their day has been. Have an honest, human moment with another human being that you normally do not engage with. It's uncomfortable, at least it is for me. I'm the biggest introvert I know. But put yourself out there. It will eventually get easier. A little any way. But you have to practice.

4) SAY HAPPY BIRTHDAY. Social media makes it unbelievably easy to keep track of birthdays for almost everyone you know. Go ahead and wish them a happy birthday on Facebook. It's a great way for you to engage and start a conversation. Take it one step further and send them a card. When's the last time you got a birthday card? I guarantee they'll remember you. (Hint: my birthday is October 1st.)

4) TAKE SOMEONE INTERESTING TO LUNCH. Reach out to someone in your network and ask them to lunch or to coffee. You don't need an agenda. Don't go in with a plan. Tell them the simple truth: that you enjoy meeting and spending time with interesting people and you'd be interested in getting to know them better.

5) INTRODUCE TWO FRIENDS. Find two friends in your network with common interests and goals who don't know each other and introduce them. It can be as easy as an email or tweet. Bob meet Jane. Jane meet Bob. I thought you two should know each other. Every connection counts, and connecting your network strengthens your network.

6) BE NICE. Always be nice.

For more info on using the power of connectivity to create opportunities in your life visit TerryLancaster.com/connect.

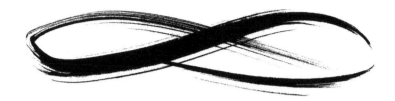

The Story You Tell The World Changes The World.

10. It's Not About You

—

Everything Is Everything.

—

"You are the average of the five people you spend the most time with."

I first heard that quote from motivational speaker Jim Rohn and took it as a warning to choose my friends wisely.

There's probably nothing that has more impact on our health, happiness and prosperity than the people we choose to surround ourselves with.

Who you associate with affects how you think, how you act, who you become. We'll accept that as a given.

Here's the part that doesn't get as much attention:

You affect the people you associate with as much as they affect you.

I ran across this great video of 32 metronomes ticking off 32 random rhythms until they gradually synch into the same frequency. It's amazing to watch. Especially the one lone hold out that struggles mightily to march to the beat of a different drummer right 'til the very end when it surrenders and syncs with the other 31. You can see it at TerryLancaster.com/NotAboutYou.

People synchronize as surely as metronomes.

I'm the captain of rec league hockey team called prophetically BEER. We named it that specifically so that when people asked who we played for we could say "I play for BEER."

And as soon as our games were over we'd head to the bar for post-game strategy sessions that usually lasted until the wee hours of the morning. Waitresses at the local watering holes would have heated arguments over who got to serve us, because we stayed a long time, drank heavily, and tipped well. A good night bringing beverages to the BEER team could pay their car note for the month.

That was then.

These days the post game celebrations for the BEER team mostly involve water, lemonade, and chef's salads.

Just like a houseful of women of childbearing age, we've synced our cycles.

Gradually, we've all mostly shifted in the same direction. Several guys I play hockey with have taken up running, working out, and generally getting their shit together. We didn't have a team meeting. We didn't change the name of the team because in all honesty, it'd be hard to fit LEMONADE AND CHEF's SALAD on the front of the jerseys.

And nobody said "Hey, let's be like Terry." It just happened. We all tuned in to the same frequency.

It happened at home too. I started attempting to live a healthier life--eating better, exercising more. And like magic, my wife and daughters began losing weight, exercising, and taking better care of themselves. Nothing makes me happier than ordering dinner in a restaurant and hearing us give our drink orders: "Water. Water. Water. Water ..."

Psychologists have a thing called confirmation bias that basically proves that we see more of what we expect to see, more of what we pay attention to.

The computer geniuses at Facebook have gone to great lengths programming an algorithm that replicates the way we experience real life. The more we "like" something, the more we interact with someone or some particular kind of post, the more stuff like that we'll see.

I've connected online with people who are committed to improving their lives. My online community is filled with self help authors and people who have made dramatic changes in their lives. One guy has lost over 200 pounds and is up at 3 every morning running eight to 10 miles. Another buddy of mine, Joey Little, has lost over 100 pounds and founded an online group, The #LiveALittle Project, which is devoted to improving lives and has exploded to 1,000 members.

And Facebook, much like life itself, is a self-perpetuating feedback loop.

The thing is, each of us is a receiver and we take in signals every day from the people around us, from what we watch on TV, from the people we interact with on Facebook. Those signal shape our thoughts and our thoughts shape our actions and our actions shape our worlds. That's how we become the average of the five people we hang out with the most.

But we're also transmitters.

Our thoughts, our actions, our realities affect everyone we connect with.

Gandhi said "Be the change you want to see in the world."

Leo Tolstoy said "Everyone thinks of changing the world, but no one thinks of changing himself."

Michael Jackson said "If you want to make the world a better place, just look at yourself and make that change."

It all starts with the man in the mirror.

No amount of bitching, whining, and tilting at windmills will ever change the world. It's too big.

But YOU can be better. You can change yourself. And changing yourself changes the world.

Living a better life, being a better you, is not just your right. It's your responsibility.

You owe it to yourself.

You owe it to your friends and family.

You owe it to the universe because we're all connected.

Everything is everything.

The first time I ever saw the diagram of an atom with the nucleus in the middle and the electrons circling around it, I remember thinking that it looked remarkably like a tiny little solar system. I'm sure I wasn't the first one to ever think that thought.

And my little junior high school brain (yes, I'm so old 7th grade was still called junior high when I went) took it a step further. What if all the atoms in the universe were just tiny little solar systems? And what if all the solar systems in the universe were just tiny little atoms in something much, much bigger. Which in turn formed themselves into solar systems which were atoms in an even bigger something. Sort of like an infinite series of Russian nesting dolls. Whoa, dude!

And of course now our understanding of what both atoms and the solar system actually look like has changed dramatically. But my seventh grade image of the universe as a set of old Russian dolls is probably closer to the way the universe actually works than we imagine.

I'm going to tell you a simple scientific fact that makes most people uncomfortable.

90% of you ain't you.

Yes, we all know that our body weight is mostly water and that we have lots of chemical and minerals and other non-living material that make up most of the vast majority of our mass.

That's not what I'm talking about.

I'm talking about organic, living creatures. Stuff that lives and dies. Breeds and multiplies. Consumes food stuff and excretes waste. I'm talking about stuff with DNA.

You're not so much a person as a walking, talking ecosystem. You are a network of parasites and bacteria and viruses joined together into the shape of a person. 90% of the living things inside of you are not human. Your skin is covered in parasites. Your mouth and your entire digestive tract are lined with bacteria. Every system in your body plays host to thousands, maybe millions of viruses all doing their thing, living their lives, going about their daily business not even knowing that you exist.

And all of us, humans, parasites, bacteria, and viruses, are depending on each other to do the right thing. To stay in balance. To keep each other alive.

I was at the doctor once a few years back and she wanted to give me an antibiotic prescription for a small sinus infection. I politely declined, because I told her it would clear up on its own in a week or so and, even though the antibiotics might clear up the infection a little sooner, I didn't like taking them and killing all my internal bacteria willy-nilly unless it was absolutely necessary. She agreed, of course, but told me she had never had anyone decline antibiotics for that reason before. Most people will load up on antibiotics to help clear up a common cold one day sooner than their body would clear it up on it's own.

It's like carpet bombing a city to fight the mosquitos.

Now I'd have a hard time selling books telling people that they need to take better care of themselves, eat more real food, exercise regularly, meditate, focus, and build better lives because they have an obligation to the parasites, bacteria, and viruses that they have living inside of them.

That's not what I'm saying.

What I'm saying is that we are the viruses.

Just like your body is an ecosystem of independent living things, all of who you are just in it for themselves.

Our families, our communities, our countries, and the Earth itself are ecosystems full of living things: us.

While we're just running around looking out for ourselves, our families, our communities, our countries, and the planet are counting on us to do the right thing, to stay in balance, to keep things in check.

Back when I cared about politics, I would describe myself as a libertarian, and I would argue with people who called on the government to help people out more economically. My favorite analogy was that of a plane that has crash landed. The plane's on fire. There's chaos and pandemonium. The best thing you can do for the sake of everyone on the plane, I would say, is calm yourself, get yourself off the plane and get the hell out of the way so everyone else can get off the plane.

I don't participate in political arguments, but I still believe that. You have an obligation to save yourself so that someone else doesn't die trying to save you.

Unfortunately, the flying ecosystem we all live on maybe crashing. It may have already crashed.

In Chapter 5, I told you about our unnecessary over-dependence on prescription pills to "manage" diseases that 20 minutes a day of exercise could cure.

One out of every five dollars spent in America is spent on health care, and we're not getting our money's worth.

If you really want to make America a better place, you don't have to vote, you don't have to write your congressman, you don't need to picket, sign a petition or sing "We Are The World" on the courthouse steps.

Get up. Get outside. And get moving.

The food you eat every day can either be the best medicine or the worst poison and it's completely and entirely up to you.

You are the only one who decides what you stock your fridge and pantry with.

You are the only one who can decide what's available for your kids when they get home from school.

My Ma caught me smoking and she said "no way." That hypocrite smokes two packs a day. -- Beastie Boys

Your kids are watching and the greatest single indicator of how their lives are going to turn out is how your life turns out.

If you go to college and get an education, it's much more likely that they will too.

If you get divorced, it's much more likely that they will, too.

If you slowly poison yourself, never exercise, get diabetes, and live your life bitching and moaning about the shitty hand life has dealt you, what do you think will happen to them?

And the rest of your family. And your friends. And your community.

We're all connected. We depend on each other.

My whole purpose in writing this book has been to convince you that you can build a better life, one better decision at a time.

I wanted to show you that change is possible no matter how old you are, no matter how broke you are, no matter how fat and out of shape you are.

You have the right to make a better life for yourself, and you have the resources to make a better life for yourself.

You don't need any fancy exercise gadgets, any expensive diet programs, or a guru on the top of a mountain to show you the path of righteousness.

You have everything you need to make your life better right now, starting right where you are. All you have to do is start.

The thing I want to leave you with is this:

You also have the responsibility to live a better life.

The fact that you are here now is a miracle beyond miracles. Life and consciousness and the ability to feel and observe and love and create are precious gifts.

You were not put in this universe to sit on the couch eating Cheetos and watching American Idol.

Carpe Diem.

Get up. Get out there and live life to the fullest.

Quit watching the tube and get busy creating a life that others want to watch.

Create a life that your family and friends want to be a part of and replicate.

Be so damn happy that when you walk in a room everyone there wants a little piece of what you've got.

You are the flame that lights the universe. Start acting like it.

Let go of all the complications that the world throws at you to distract you from your one and only purpose on this planet: To live the one and only life you've been given BETTER.

That's all you've got.

That's all you can do.

And that's enough.

At the end of the day being a better YOU is your full time job.

Now get to work.

ACTION STEPS

1) TAKE YOUR FAMILY FOR A WALK. Beg. Plead. Cajole. Threaten to disconnect the cable and change the Wi-Fi password. Do whatever you have to do to get your loved ones up off the couch, outside in the sunshine and moving. One foot in front of the other.

2) CLEAN OUT YOUR PANTRY. Go open up your pantry door and take a look inside. Is it real food or real crap? Throw away all the pre-packaged, edible food-like substances. All the crackers and cookies. All the low fat, low sugar, diet industry junk you've been sold through the years. All the stealth sugar delivery systems that have snuck into your home. All the soda. All the snacks. If it's not in your house, your kids can't eat it.

3) STOCK UP. Now that you've got room, go buy some real food. Stuff that doesn't need a label to tell you what it is. Stuff that used to be alive. Stuff that rots: that's how you know it's real food.

4) COOK A FAMILY DINNER. Cook the real food in a real oven over the real stove and sit down to eat a real meal with your real family and have a real conversation. No TV. No cell phones. No takeout.

5) BRAG ONLINE. Put pictures on Pinterest of the awesome, colorful real meal you've prepared. Tweet on the Twitter about how many days in a row you've been walking, running, or doing pushups #DontBreakTheStreak. Post on Facebook before and after pictures of you and the 20 pounds you've lost. Talking about it in public commits you and motivates others. You can do it. They can, too, if you'll just help each other.

6) HELP ME SPREAD THE WORD. If what I've written makes sense to you and has encouraged you in anyway to build a better life, please help me spread the word. You have all the power. Online reviews are the primary factor affecting book sales in today's economy. You can change the world just sharing your story. It doesn't have to be Shakespeare. And it doesn't have to be the five paragraph book report you hated so much from high school. Just visit TerryLancaster.com/review and write a quick two-line, 50-word review that says what you liked about this book and how you think others can benefit from reading it.

For more info on how improving your life improves the lives of others visit TerryLancaster.com/NotAboutYou.

TERRY LANCASTER

WILL YOU DO ME A FAVOR?

I know I already asked, but I can't begin to emphasize how important it is for you to write a brief two-line, 50-word review letting everyone know what you thought about **BETTER! Self Help For The Rest Of Us.**

Your opinion matters.

Back in the olden days, a couple of editors in New York wearing grey flannel suits were the only ones who could decide what books got published and what books were read by the public. Today, thousands of books are published every day. And what you say about them in online reviews are the deciding factor in whether or not they ever get read.

Please visit TerryLancaster.com/review and leave a brief note telling what you liked about the book and what you think could be of benefit to other readers.

I'd love it if every review were a five-star review, so don't be bashful. If you feel the book only deserves four stars, I guess I could live with that too. But even if you think this was all pointless drivel and I couldn't write my way out of a paper bag, go ahead and let everyone know what you think. Your opinion matters whether I like it or not

Two lines. Fifty words. That's all I ask!

Visit TerryLancaster.com/review

Thank you so very much. I'll name my firstborn son after you!

Made in the USA
Columbia, SC
25 January 2021